FAVOURITES FROM THE KITCHEN

OF

MARION SHEEHY

A cookbook

THESE ARE MY FAVOURITE TRIED AND TRUE RECIPES. MY HUSBAND, JOHN, HELPED ME PUT THEM TOGETHER. I PROMISE NO INGREDIENT HAS BEEN LEFT OUT.

WE HOPE YOU ENJOY LOOKING THROUGH THE COOKBOOK AND TRYING SOME OF THE RECIPES. IT IS IN NO WAY A PROFESSIONAL JOB, JUST A LABOR OF LOVE.

BUEN PROVECHO!!!

2017
ELDEN PUBLISHING
ATLANTA, GEORGIA

ISBN-13: 978-0-9789271-7-2
ISBN-10: 0-9789271-7-6

Library of Congress Control Number: 2017950529

Edited by Susanna Sheehy

Published by Elden Publishing LLC, Atlanta, Georgia

Thanks to Mary Castro for photographs used in the book.

Table of Contents

Desserts....................................155

Miscellaneous.......................169

Appetizers

Antipasto Augustino

Betty Bono - Guatemala

I always asked Betty for this recipe. It was one she brought to the wonderful parties in San Luis. It was always gobbled up quickly. She said she would give it to me whenever I left Guatemala. Sure enough, the day we left she appeared at the airport with it. As good as it is, I'd have given up the recipe to have stayed in Guatemala.

1	Leek
1	Onion
1	Tomato
2	Tablespoons Parsley
1/4	Cup Parmesan Cheese
1	Teaspoon Salt
	Freshly ground Pepper
3	Tablespoons Olive Oil

- Cook the vegetables slowly in hot olive oil until tender. Stir so they don't burn.
- Add ¼ Cup Parmesan Cheese, 1 teaspoon salt, and freshly ground pepper to taste.
- Serve on toasted rounds of Bread.

You can double this as it is really good and is great on French bread for Lunch.

Zucchini Appetizers

Heat Oven to 350°

Spray 13" x 9" x 2"

1	Cup Bisquick Mix
1/2	Cup Finely Chopped Onion
1/2	Cup Parmesan Cheese
2	Tablespoons chopped Parsley
1/2	Teaspoon Seasoned Salt
12	Teaspoons Oregano
1/2	Teaspoon Pepper
1	Clove Garlic, minced
1/4	Cup Vegetable Oil
4	Beaten Eggs
3	Cups Zucchini, thinly sliced

- Combine all ingredients except the zucchini. Mix well.
- Add zucchini and blend
- Spread in Prepared Pan
- Bake for 25 minutes or until golden

A good way to use up the zucchini your neighbor gives you. It's delicious, too.

Mushroom Puffs

It makes about 50 puffs. These can be frozen before baking so are handy to have in freezer. Allow extra time for baking when frozen. If you make them bigger they are good for lunch, too.

Pastry

3   Ounces Cream Cheese, Softened

1/2   Cup Butter, Softened

1 1/2 Cups Flour

- Mix Cheese and Butter together. Stir in flour. Blend well and Chill.

(Continued)

Filling

1	Onion
3	Tablespoons Butter
1/2	Pound Fresh Mushrooms, Minced
1/4	Teaspoon Thyme
1/2	Teaspoon Salt
	Pepper to taste
1	Tablespoon Flour
1/4	Cup Sour Cream

- Sauté onions in butter until soft and transparent.
- Add mushrooms and cook 3 minutes.
- Add seasonings, mix well.
- Sprinkle flour over mixture and add sour cream.
- Cook until thickened. Do not boil.
- Roll chilled dough on floured board until thin.
- Cut into 3-inch rounds and place a teaspoon of filling on each.
- Fold edges over and press together. Prick with fork.
- Heat oven to 450°.
- Bake on ungreased sheet for 15 minutes.

Ham and Cheese Appetizers

- Heat oven to 350°
- Spray 13" x 9" x 2" pan with cooking spray

2	Cups Bisquick Baking Mix
3/4	Cup Ham, Chopped
1	Cup Shredded Swiss or Cheddar Cheese (about 4 ounces)
1/2	Cup Onion, Finely Chopped
1/2	Cup Sour Cream
2	Tablespoons Parsley, Chopped
2	Cloves Garlic, Minced
2/3	Cup Milk
1	Egg

- Mix all ingredients and spread in prepared pan.
- Bake 25 to 30 minutes or until golden brown.
- Cut into rectangles.

Makes about 36 appetizers. Great for coffees. Nice for lunch, too.

Olive Cheese Balls

2	Cups Sharp Cheddar Cheese, Grated
1 1/4	Cups Flour
1/2	Cup Butter or Margarine, Melted
36	Small Pimento Stuffed Olives, Drained

- Mix Cheese, flour, and butter until blended.
- Mold 1 teaspoon of dough around each olive.
- Refrigerate for 1 hour.
- Bake for 15 to 20 minutes in a 400° oven.

These are great, but warn guests if you serve them out of the oven as the olive stays hot.

Cheese Wafers

Heat oven to 300°

1	Pound Cheddar Cheese, Grated
1	Teaspoon Salt
1/2	Teaspoon Red Pepper
3	Cups Flour
2 1/2	Sticks Butter, Creamed

- Mix cheese, salt, pepper, and flour into creamed butter with hands.
- Mold into small balls and place on an ungreased cookie sheet. Press each ball into a wafer with a floured fork.
- Bake for 20 to 30 minutes. Be careful not to over brown.
- Remove from sheet and cool.

Makes about 3 dozen. Keep them in a tight container. They can be frozen.

Ceviche

Mary Sheehy – Costa Rica

1 1/2	Pounds white fish fillet such as Sea Bass or Small or Large Mouth Bass for you fisherman. I make it with 3 pounds of cooked shrimp.
1 1/4	Cup of Fresh Lime Juice (Do not use Lemons)
1/2	Cup Parsley, Finely Chopped
1/2	Pounds Onions, Finely Chopped
1	Tablespoon Worcestershire Sauce
2	Tablespoons Oil
	A few drops of Tabasco
2	Teaspoons Salt
	Dash of pepper, Some whole Peppercorns and Cloves

(Continued)

- Wash fish fillets and cut into small pieces (about 1/4 to 1/2 inch). Make sure all bones are removed.Put in large glass or ceramic bowl.
- Add Lime Juice (not Lemon) and the rest of the ingredients.
- Cover and keep in the refrigerator. Serve the next day.

It usually needs 24 hours. If you use cooked shrimp less time is needed. The flavor of the marinade is better if left longer. It's a great starter to a dinner served with saltine crackers. You can add chopped tomatoes if you want.

Ceviche is a national dish from Peru but is served in most of Central and South America. The original is the "White Ceviche" as described above.

You can adapt this recipe to any kind of fish or shellfish. Always make sure the fish is fresh. Buen Provecho!

There is a controversy as to where this recipe originated. Mary Sheehy says it is hers and she gave it to Wes. Fred Says it is Mary's. We got it from Wes. No matter what, it's absolutely the best.

Crab and Artichoke Dip

Oven 350°

8	Ounces cooked Crab Meat, Canned or Fresh
2	Small cans Artichoke Hearts, Drained and Quartered
8	Ounces Cream Cheese, Softened
1/2	Cup Mayonnaise
1/2	Cup Parmesan cheese
2	Cloves Garlic, Minced
	Pinch of Dill Weed

- Combine cheese, Mayonnaise, Parmesan, Garlic, and Dill. Mix well.
- Stir in Crab Meat and Artichokes.
- Bake in small oven-proof casserole for 25 to 30 minutes.
- Serve warm with Crackers.

Oyster Roll

16	Ounces of Cream Cheese, softened
2	Tablespoons Mayonnaise
2	Teaspoons Worcestershire Sauce
3/4	Teaspoon Garlic Salt
2	Cans Smoked Oysters, drained and chopped

- Mix first 4 ingredients, blending well.
- Spray a piece of wax paper about 15 inches with cooking spray.
- Spread the cheese mix on the wax paper forming a 10 x 6 inch rectangle.
- Put chopped Oysters on top.
- Roll as you would a Jelly Roll.
- Chill in the refrigerator until ready to serve.
- Unroll and garnish with chopped parsley and lemon slices and serve with Melba Toast.

Even those who don't like Oysters like this, and you can half it if you are serving a small group. It will serve more than 12.

Shrimp Remoulade

Betty Bono - Guatemala

1 1/2	Pounds cooked, peeled Shrimp
1	Cup Onion, minced
1	Cup Parsley, minced

- Put these 3 ingredients in a bowl and mix well. Set aside
- In a saucepan. Heat together:

2/3	Cup Salad Oil
1/3	Cup Vinegar
1	Clove Garlic, minced
1 1/2	Teaspoons Salt
	Freshly ground Pepper to taste

- When hot pour over shrimp and stir
- Put in refrigerator to cool.

I used to serve this with small plates and crackers as an appetizer. It is really good. It also could be served as a first course on a bed of lettuce.

Onion Rounds

2/3   Cup Mayonnaise

1/2   Cup Parmesan Cheese

1   Small Onion, finely chopped (processor is good here)

           Miniature Rye bread or cut rounds of white bread

           Paprika

- Heat oven to broil.
- Combine all ingredients except Bread and Paprika.
- Spread on top of Bread Rounds.
- Top each with Paprika.
- Place slices on greased cookie sheet and broil 6 inches from heat.
- Watch them as it only takes about a minute.
- Serve hot.

You can make these ahead and broil just before serving. I use a loaf of white bread and cut rounds with a biscuit cutter. Everyone loves these and they are a quick boca as you usually have the ingredients on hand.

Crab Mold

1	Can Tomato Soup
1	Envelope Plain Gelatin
8	Ounces Cream Cheese, softened
8	Ounces Crab Meat, checked for shell
1/3	Cup each finely chopped Onion, finely chopped Green Pepper and finely chopped Celery
1	Cup Mayonnaise

- Heat tomato Soup and dissolve the Gelatin in it.
- Blend in Cheese and other ingredients
- Mix until blended. You should not see any white of the Cheese.
- Place in mold and chill until firm. I put a bit of cooking spray in the mold.
- Unmold carefully and serve with crackers or Melba Toast.

Asparagus Rollups

20	Slices of very soft white bread with the crust removed
1	Package (8 ounces) Cream Cheese, softened
4	Ounces Blue Cheese, crumbled
1	Egg
	Dash Tabasco
	Dash of Worcestershire Sauce
1	Can (14 1/2 ounces) Asparagus spears, well drained
1/2	Cup melted Butter

- Flatten the bread slices by rolling one or two times with a rolling pin.
- Combine cheeses, egg, Tabasco, and Worcestershire sauce.
- Spread this mixture evenly over each bread slice.
- Place one Asparagus spear on each slice and roll up.
- If the spear is too long, trim, and save overhang pieces for another rollup.

(Continued)

- Dip each rollup into Butter and cut into thirds.
- Place each piece on ungreased cookie sheet
- Bake the rollups at 425° for 15 minutes or until golden. Serve hot. Makes 5 dozen.

If you're not serving them right away, the rollups can be frozen and reheated using regular baking instructions. Nice to have in the freezer as everyone loves them, even people who don't like blue cheese like them!

Hot Crab Spread

- Preheat oven to 375°

16	Ounces Cream Cheese, softened
2	Tablespoons Milk
1/4	Cup finely chopped Onion
	Salt and Pepper to taste
1	Teaspoon chopped Parsley
1	Can (16 ounces) Crab Meat, flaked, shell and cartilage removed
	Dash of Tabasco Sauce
	Dash of Worcestershire
2	Tablespoons chopped Chives
1/3	Cup Blanched Slivered Almonds (optional)

- Combine all ingredients except Almonds and blend well.
- Put in an oven proof dish and bake until bubbly, about 15 minutes.
- If you are using almonds, sprinkle over mixture just before serving.
- You can keep the mixture warm in a chafing dish or serve it as it comes out of the oven with fresh vegetables or Melba toast.

It is delicious! I love it cold the next day. It can be cut in half to serve a smaller crowd. Serves about 12 for Bocas

Salads

Thai Chicken Pasta Salad

1	Pound Spaghetti Pasta
3/4	Cup Soy Sauce
1/4	Cup Peanut Oil
2	Cup Mayonnaise
1	Tablespoon Dijon Mustard
1/4	Cup Sesame Oil
2	Whole Chicken Breasts, cooked and cut into large chunks
6	Green Onions, thinly sliced
2	Carrots, peeled and chopped
1	Red Bell Pepper, chopped
1	8 ounce can Bamboo Shoots, drained
1/2	Cup Chopped Cilantro
1	Tablespoon Toasted Sesame Seeds

- Cook Noodles, drain, and add 1/2 cup of the Soy Sauce and all of the Peanut Oil. Marinate noodles while cutting other ingredients.
- Mix together the Mayonnaise, Mustard, Sesame Oil, and remaining soy sauce. Mix with the remaining ingredients.
- Add this mixture to the noodles.
- Garnish with toasted Sesame Seeds.

This is best if made the day before.

Five Green Salad with Yogurt Dressing

1/2	Cup Olive or Salad Oil
1/4	Cup Red Wine Vinegar
1	Tablespoon Sugar
2	Tablespoons Low fat Yogurt
2	Tablespoons Dijon Mustard with Seeds
1	Teaspoon dried Parsley Flakes
1	Teaspoon Salt
1/4	Teaspoon coarsely Ground Pepper
16	Cups loosely packed mixed Salad Greens

- In a large bowl mix the first 8 ingredients together
- Pour the dressing over the salad greens and toss gently to coat well.

It makes 8 accompaniment servings. This dressing is very good and nice on Tomatoes, too.

Won Ton Salad

1	Green onion, Chopped (use two inches green part)
1	Clove Garlic, Quartered
1/4	Cup Soy Sauce
1/4	Cup White Wine Vinnegar
2	Teaspoons Sugar
1	Teaspoon Dry Mustard
1/4	Teaspoon Fresh Ginger or 1/2 Teaspoon Powdered Ginger
1	Teaspoon Worcestershire Sauce
1/4	Cup Peanut Oil
2	Tablespoons Sesame Oil (This gives the flavor)
1/4	Cup Sesame Seeds, Toasted

- Mince Onion and Garlic in Food Processor.
- Blend in vinegar, Soy Sauce, Sugar, Mustard, Ginger and Worcestershire with machine running.
- Gradually add Peanut and Sesame Oil.
- Remove from machine and stir in Sesame Seeds.

This can be made a day ahead.

(Continued)

Salad

1/4	Pound Cooked Chicken Breast Meat Cut into 1" Pieces
1/4	Pound Smoked Ham Cut into Strips
1 1/2	Cups Water Chestnuts, Sliced and Drained
	Red Lettuce in Pieces
1	Pound Spinach in Pieces
1/2	Can Bean Sprouts

- Combine all ingredients except Bean Sprouts in a large bowl and toss with enough dressing to coat. Top with Bean Sprouts and Wonton Strips.
- Pass remaining dressing separately.

This is a great salad and everyone loves it. I don't add the Bean Sprouts.

It serves 8. It can easily serve more by adding extra salad ingredients)

Cranberry Waldorf Salad

- Grease a 1 1/2 quart ring mold with cooking spray.

2	1 ounce packages Unflavored Gelatin
1	Cup Orange Juice
2	(16 ounce) Cans Whole Berry Cranberry Sauce
3/4	Cup Apples, peeled and chopped
3/4	Cup Celery, chopped
3/4	Cup Walnuts, chopped

- Mix Gelatin and Orange Juice. Set aside for 5 minutes.
- Place over low heat and stir until Gelatin is dissolved.
- Remove from heat and pour into large bowl with Cranberry Sauce. Stir well.
- Chill until partially set.
- Fold in Apples, Celery, and Walnuts.
- Pour into prepared mold and chill until firm.
- Unmold carefully.

This is lovely at the holidays, but good any time. It's wonderful with Turkey or Chicken. Even Men who don't like Gelatin Salads like this. Serves 8

Corn Salad

2	(12 ounce) Cans White Shoepeg Corn, drained
3/4	Cup Cucumber, diced
1/4	Cup Onion, diced
1 to 2	Medium Tomatoes, diced

* Mix the vegetables together.

Dressing

1/2	Cup Sour Cream
2	Tablespoons Vinegar
4	Tablespoons Mayonnaise
2	Teaspoons Salt (I use one)
1/2	Teaspoon Dry Mustard
1/2	Teaspoon Pepper

* Mix the ingredients and pour over the corn mixture. Serve cold

Serves 8 and is really good.

Apple Slaw

1/2   Cup Mayonnaise

2   Tablespoons Honey

1 1/2   Tablespoons Fresh Lime Juice

1 1/2   Teaspoons Kosher Salt. This really is right in this salad.

1/2   Teaspoon freshly ground Pepper

- In a small bowl, mix the above ingredients. This can be made ahead and refrigerated for up to 2 days.

1   Cup Pecans, toasted in a 400° oven for about 5 minutes or until fragrant. Allow to cool. Set aside.

4   Cups cabbage, finely shredded

3   Medium Granny Smith Apples, coarsely shredded. I chop them in small pieces.

3   Medium Carrots, coarsely shredded

2   Medium Red Peppers, thinly sliced

1/2   Cups coarsely chopped Chives

- Combine Vegetables, except chives. Just before serving add the dressing, pecans, chives, and toss well.

This serves 10 and is very good with a pork dinner. It's a nice change from regular slaw.

Spinach Salad

Del Wheelock – Sebastopol, California

Salad

Spinach, washed, dried, and torn into pieces.
Red Onion, thinly sliced
Mushrooms, sliced
Bacon, fried crisply and crumbled
Hard boiled eggs, cut up

- Mix these ingredients together gently.

(Continued)

Dressing

2/3	Cup Salad Oil
1/4	Cup Wine Vinegar
2	Tablespoons Soy Sauce
1	Teaspoon Dry Mustard
1/2	Teaspoon Curry
1/2	Teaspoon each salt and pepper

- Mix together well and pour over salad.

I haven't given any amounts on the salad as this depends on the number of servings needed. The dressing keeps if you don't need it all at once.

This is a delicious salad and even non-spinach lovers like it.

Black Bean Salsa

1	Can Black Beans, drained
1	Red Pepper, diced
1	Green Pepper, diced
1	Red Onion, finely chopped, not minced, but not too course
2	Tomatoes, chopped
3	Ears of freshly cooked corn cut from cob (I use a can of Kernel Corn, drained and find it tastes good, too, and is easier.
1	Jalapeño, thinly sliced (beware of the seeds as they are hot and wash your hands after cutting Pepper) This can be omitted as sometimes people get a piece of it and go through the roof!
1/3	Cup Cilantro, chopped
1/3	Cup Olive Oil
1/3	Cup Lime Juice (not Lemon)
1	Teaspoon Salt
1/2	Teaspoon Pepper
1/2	Teaspoon Ground Cumin
	Dash of Cayenne Pepper

(Continued)

- Mix together and let stand at least an hour.

If you refrigerate it return it to room temperature before serving. This is a real crowd pleaser.

Fire and Ice Tomatoes

6	Large Ripe Tomatoes
1	Large Green Pepper
1	Large Red Onion
3/4	Cup Vinegar
1 1/2	Teaspoons Celery Salt
4 1/2	Teaspoons Sugar
1/8	Teaspoon Mustard Seed
1/2	Teaspoon Salt
1/8	Teaspoon Cayenne
1/8	Teaspoon black Pepper
1/4	Cup Cold Water
1	Cucumber, sliced

- Skin Tomatoes and cut into quarters.
- Slice Pepper in strips.
- Cut onion into rings.
- Arrange the vegetables attractively on a serving platter, each separate from the other. (Platter should have an edge as the sauce will be poured over the vegetables)
- Combine the rest of the ingredients (except the Cucumber) in a sauce pan and bring to a boil.

(Continued)

- Boil furiously for one minute.
- Pour over the vegetables, cool slightly, and refrigerate until cold.
- Just before serving arrange the sliced Cucumber over the other vegetables.

Makes 6 to 8 servings and has a little bite to it.

Chicken Salad with Curry Mayonnaise

2 to 2 1/2   Cups diced cooked Chicken

1   Cup Celery, diced

1   Teaspoon Fresh Dill,
                chopped

- Mix together well.

(Continued)

Curry Mayonnaise

1 1/2 to 2	Teaspoons Curry Powder
3/4	Cup Mayonnaise
1	Tablespoon Lemon Juice
1/2	Cup Heavy Cream

- Stir Curry into Mayonnaise. Add the Lemon Juice
- Check the seasoning before adding more curry.
- Fold in Cream.
- Spoon over Chicken and toss lightly.
- Chill through before serving.

This is a truly delicious salad. It'd great for a luncheon.

SOUPS

Mushroom Soup

Barbara Chelton – Atlanta

2	Cups chopped Onion
2	Tablespoons Butter (Canola Oil for low fat version)
3/4	Cup sliced Mushrooms
1/2	Cup Dry White Wine
2	Tablespoons dried Dill
1	Tablespoon Sweet Hungarian Paprika
1	Tablespoon Soy Sauce

- In sauce pan cook the Onion in Butter until softened.
- Add the Mushrooms and remaining ingredients.
- Simmer the mixture, covered for 15 minutes stirring occasionally.
- In another sauce pan:

2	Tablespoons Butter
3	Tablespoons Flour
1	Cup Milk (No fat Buttermilk)
1 1/2	Cups Chicken Broth
1/2	Cup Sour Cream (No fat Sour Cream or Cream Cheese)

(Continued)

- Melt Butter and stir in Flour. Cook roux over low heat for 3 minutes.
- Remove pan from heat and whisk in Milk.
- Return pan to low heat, whisking until mixture thickens.
- Add mushroom mixture to the Milk mixture and add the Broth.
- Simmer for 15 minutes, stirring occasionally.

Remove from heat and stir in Sour Cream. Serves 8

We had the low-fat version and it was delicious.

Tomato Consommé

4	Cups Chicken Broth
16	Ounce Can Plum Tomatoes, Chopped fine with the juice
2	Teaspoons Tomato Paste
1/2	Teaspoon Thyme
1/2	Teaspoon Basil
2	Teaspoons Lemon Juice
2	Tablespoons Sherry or Madeira

• Place all the ingredients except the Sherry in a sauce pan.
• Simmer for 15 minutes.
• Add the Sherry and serve garnished with chopped Chives or Parsley.

This is very good and easy. A nice start to a dinner. Serves 6

Black Bean Soup

1 1/2	Cups Black Beans soaked for 4 hours, drained, and rinsed.
1	Yellow Onions, finely chopped
2	Stalks of Celery, finely chopped
2	Tablespoons Butter
1/2	Teaspoon Thyme
3	Sprigs Parsley
8	Cups Chicken Broth
	Juice of half a Lemon
1/4	Cup Sherry

(Continued)

- In large pot, sauté Onion in Butter until softened. (do not brown) Add the celery and sauté for 3 minutes.
- Add the beans, bay leaf, thyme, parsley sprigs and broth. Cover and simmer for 1 1/2 hours or until beans are tender. Discard Bay leaf and Parsley.
- Puree half of the mixture in a blender.
- Return to the remaining Beans in saucepan.
- Heat to simmering and add lemon juice and sherry.

Serve hot with a garnish of finely chopped hard boiled eggs, and chopped parsley. Add a thick slice of lemon to each bowl. Great for lunch with a Cuban sandwich! Serves 8.

Seafood Chowder

1	13 Ounce can of Lump Crab
8	Ounces Small Cooked Shrimp or Canned Shrimp
1	Can Minced Clams
4	Strips Bacon, diced. You can use Hormel Cooked and Crumbled
1	Clove Fresh Garlic, minced
2	Potatoes, diced and cooked
2	Teaspoons Salt
1/8	Teaspoon Pepper
1/2	Teaspoon Spice Island Fine Herbs or equivalent Herb Mix
1	16 ounce can Cream Style Corn
3	Cups Milk
1	Can Chicken Broth
1/2	Cup chopped Green Onion
2	Tablespoons minced Parsley or dry equivalent

- Heat all ingredients but do not boil!
- Optional 1 cup White Wine.

I cooked the potatoes with chopped leeks and added them to the mix instead of the green onions. It was good, too. Serves 6-8

New England Clam Chowder

1   Quart Soft Shelled Clams **or**

2   7 1/2 Ounce Cans of Minced Clams, drained reserving the broth

- If using fresh clams scrub and soak the clams in three waters to remove the sand.
- Steam over cup of water for 8 minutes until shells open.
- Strain the broth through cheese cloth to remove any sand.
- Set aside the clams and reserve the broth.

3   Small Potatoes, peeled and diced

1   Medium Yellow Onion, finely chopped

3   Slices Bacon cut into small pieces

3   Cups Milk

1   Cup Heavy Cream

1   Tablespoon Butter

         Salt if necessary

         Freshly ground Black Pepper

(Continued)

- Boil the potatoes in salted water for 15 minutes.
- Fry bacon until 1 tablespoon of fat is rendered.
- Remove bacon and saljte onion in fat for 3 minutes
- Add clam broth or broth from canned clams. Simmer for 5 minutes.
- Add the chopped clams, milk, butter, cream and drained potatoes.
- Season with salt if necessary.
- Simmer until potatoes are just tender
- Serve with a sprinkling of freshly ground black pepper and reserved bacon.

Carrot Vichyssoise

Khartoum, Sudan

2	Potatoes, peeled and diced
1 1/4	Cups Carrots, peeled and sliced
3	Cups Chicken Broth

- Put in pot and bring to a boil. Simmer until vegetables are tender.
- Puree until smooth.
- Put in a mixing bowl
- To the puree of vegetables add:

A pinch of White Pepper
1 Cup of heavy Cream or Crème Fraiche

- Stir chilled.
- Serve in chilled bowls. Garnish with grated Carrot.

Gazpacho

6	Small ripe Tomatoes cut into pieces, seeds removed
1/2	Medium sized Green Pepper cut into small pieces
1	Small Cucumber, peeled and cut into small pieces
6	Thin Scallions cut into small pieces

- Place the cut vegetables in a bowl

Dressing

1	Garlic Clove, minced
1/2	Teaspoon Salt
	Freshly ground Black Pepper
2	Tablespoons Lemon Juice
6	Tablespoons Salad Oil
2	Tablespoons chopped Parsley
2	Tablespoons finely chopped fresh Basil or 1/2 Teaspoon dried

- Before serving add to vegetable mixture

1/2	Cup cold Chicken Broth
1/2	Cup chilled Tomato Juice

This was served to rave reviews, and I do think it is the best Gazpacho I have tasted

CASSEROLES

Manicotti

This is made with crepes and it is delicious and worth the trouble. As the book says, real Manicotti is made with crepes not those starchy shells you buy!

Crepes

1 1/4	Cups Water
5	Eggs
1 1/4	Cup Flour
	Pinch of Salt
1	Teaspoon Melted Butter
	Additional melted Butter to make Crepes

(Continued))

- To make Crepes place Water, Eggs, Flour, Salt, and Melted Butter into a blender and blend until smooth.
- Heat a 7 to 8 inch Crepe Pan (I use the non stick small skillet that size). Brush with Melted Butter.
- Pour in enough batter to cover the bottom of the pan. This is about 3 Tablespoons. I found it was good to measure it as you sometimes make them too thick. 3 tablespoons are a little less than 1/4 cup.
- Cook Crepe until dry on top. Do not let them brown. Turn Crepe and cook until dry, about 30 seconds.
- Remove Crepes to wire rack and repeat process. You can stack the Crepes as they don't stick together.

You should have about 30 Crepes. One Time I didn't measure the batter and ended up with only 19. They weren't so hot. You get into a groove and it goes fast.

(Continued)

Sauce

1/4	Cup Olive Oil (I use less)
1	Cup Finely Chopped Onion
1	Clove Crushed Garlic
1	Large Can Plus 1 Small Can of Italian Plum Tomatoes, with the liquid.
1	6 Ounce Can Tomato Paste
3	Tablespoons Chopped Parsley
2 1/4	Teaspoons Sugar
1 1/2	Teaspoons Oregano
1/2	Teaspoon Basil
1/2	Teaspoon Salt
	Freshly Ground Pepper to Taste

- Heat the oil. Sauté the Onions and Garlic. Add all the remaining ingredients and simmer covered for 1 hour.

This can be used in any dish calling for Marinara Sauce and it freezes well, too.

(Continued)

Filling for Crepes

2	Pounds Ricotta Cheese
1/2	Pound Diced Mozzarella Cheese
1/2	Cup Parmesan Cheese, divided
2	Tablespoons Chopped Parsley
	Salt and Pepper to Taste

- In a large bowl combine the Ricotta, Mozzarella, and 1/3 Cup of the Parmesan. Add the Parsley, Salt, and Pepper.

To Assemble the Casserole:

- Pour some sauce in the bottom of a shallow baking dish.
- Put about 1 1/2 tablespoons of the Cheese Filling in each Crepe. Fold in Thirds and Place it seam side down in the baking dish.
- Cover the Crepes with the remaining sauce and sprinkle with the remaining Parmesan. It can be refrigerated at this point or frozen.
- Bake uncovered for 30 minutes in 350° oven. Cool for 5 minutes before serving. If frozen bake for 1 hour in 350° oven.

Serve this with salad and Italian bread. No one will miss the meat!

Mushroom Quiche

1	9" Pie Shell
4	Eggs, beaten
1/2	Pound Fresh Sliced Mushrooms
1/4	Cup Sliced Green Onions. (I use regular onions if green aren't on hand)
1	Tablespoon Butter
1	Cup (4 Ounces) Shredded Swiss Cheese (Any good Cheese will do).
1	Cup of Half-n-Half, Light Cream, or Whole Milk
1/4	Cup Grated Parmesan Cheese
1/2	Teaspoon Salt
1/8	Teaspoon Pepper

- Sauté the Onion and Mushrooms in the Butter until the Mushrooms are lightly browned and the onions are tender, about 6 - 8 Minutes.
- Stir together the Swiss Cheese and Mushroom Mix. Put it into the baked Pie Shell.

(Continued)

- To the beaten Eggs add all the rest of the ingredients. Beat it until well blended. Pour it over the Mushroom Mix.
- Bake in preheated oven 30 to 40 minutes or until a knife inserted near the center comes out clean.
- Let it stand for 5 minutes before serving.

I like this as you usually have the ingredients on hand. It makes an easy dinner with a salad.

Spinach Timbale

The first time we tried this, my son Michael made it. He did a good job and it became a favorite. The next time, though, I did it with fewer pans!

1/2	Cup Finely Chopped Onions
5	Tablespoons Butter
2/3	Cup Plus 2 tablespoons Bread Crumbs
1/2	Cup Gruyere or Swiss Cheese, Grated
1/2	Teaspoon Salt
1/8	Teaspoon Nutmeg
	Cayenne to Taste
5	Eggs
1	Cup Milk
3	Cups Chopped Cooked Spinach
3	Eggs, hard boiled (optional)

- Cook the Onions in 1 Tablespoon of the Butter over low heat for 10 minutes. Do not let them color.
- Combine the Onions and 2/3 Cup Bread Crumbs, Cheese, Salt, Nutmeg and Cayenne. Beat in the Eggs one at a time.

(Continued)

- Heat the remaining Butter with the Milk until the Butter is melted and the Milk is hot. Gradually add to the Egg and Cheese mixture.
- Fold in the Spinach and pour the mixture into a 1 1/2 quart Buttered Mold. (I use cooking spray)
- Set the mold in a pan of boiling water and bake it in a 325° oven for 35 to 45 minutes depending on the depth of mold or until a knife comes out clean when inserted in the center.
- Remove the mold from the water and let it stand for 5 minutes.
- Run the knife around the edge and turn out on a platter.
- Cover the top with chopped hardboiled Egg if desired.
- Serve with melted Butter and Lemon Juice. (This I have never done, but it's in the recipe. Maybe I'm missing something) It can be cut from the mold like a pie to serve, too.

It is very good and a lovely side dish or a meal in itself with a salad. It's good cold, too!

Torta Rustica

Gretchen Reese

This is really great and worth the time.

1	Tablespoon Butter
1	Medium Onion, finely chopped
1	Tablespoon Minced Garlic
2	10 ounce packages frozen chopped Spinach, thawed and squeezed dry
8	Ounces Ricotta Cheese, drained
4	Eggs, lightly beaten
1	17 ounce package frozen Puff Pastry
2	13 ounce jars of Artichoke Hearts, well drained
10	Ounces thinly sliced Deli Ham or Prosciutto
10	Ounces thinly sliced Provolone Cheese
2	7 Ounce Jars of Roasted Red Peppers, well drained
3/4	Cup Plain Bread Crumbs, divided
1	Egg, lightly beaten with 1 Teaspoon Water for Glaze

(Continued)

- In a small skillet over medium low heat melt the Butter, add the Onion and Garlic. Sauté until tender.
- In a large bowl stir together the Onion, Garlic, Spinach, Ricotta Cheese, and Eggs. Set aside.
- Thaw one 17 ounce package of frozen Puff Pastry Sheets at room temperature for about 20 minutes. It should be cold when it's worked.
- Preheat the oven to 425° spray a 1 inch spring form pan with cooking spray.
- On a lightly floured board roll one sheet of Puff Pastry into a rectangle about 11" by 13". Fold the corners over to make a square. Cut with a sharp knife and reserve the scraps.
- Place the square of dough in the bottom of the spring form pan so it comes up the sides at least an inch.
- Roll the second sheet and make the square. Set aside for Torta top.
- Use the scraps to fill in the empty sides of the pan. The dough should overlap at least 1/2 inch all the way around. Brush well with melted butter.
- Divide the Artichokes, Ham, Cheese, Red Peppers, and Spinach Mixture into two equal parts.
- Layer the Ham in the bottom so it covers it.
- Sprinkle with 2 Tablespoons Crumbs.
- Add a Layer of Pepper and 2 Tablespoons of Crumbs.
- Press half the Spinach mixture on top of the Peppers
- Press half the Artichokes into the Spinach and top it with the remaining Spinach Mixture.
- Layer Ham, Crumbs, Artichokes, Red Peppers and Crumbs as before.
- Brush Egg wash around the edge of the Pastry and place the square of Dough on the top.
- Cut off all but 1/2 inch of the excess Dough.

(Continued)

57

- Brush more Egg wash around the edge of the circle, pinch the edges together and roll toward the Torta. Brush the whole top with the Egg wash.
- Prick the top of Pastry twice in the center.
- Bake at 425° for 10 minutes and 375° for the remaining 45 minutes.
- Allow to cool at room temperature for an hour before slicing.
- Serve with seasoned tomato Sauce or Marinara Sauce.

The secret is to have all the ingredients ready and just do it step by step. Serves 6

Four Bean Casserole

Susanna Sheehy

1	Can Lima Beans, drained
1	Can Kidney Beans, drained
1	Can Pork and Beans, not drained
1	Can Green Beans, drained
3/4	Pound Bacon Diced and Fried
4	Large Onions Chopped
1/3	Cup Vinegar
3/4	Cup Brown Sugar
1	Tablespoon Dry Mustard

- Cook Bacon, Onion, Vinegar, Brown Sugar and Mustard Powder together. Simmer 20 minutes.
- Add all the beans and bake for 3 hours.
- Oven 325° for 3 hours

This is delicious and you can't beat it with Potato Salad and all those good things that go with a Bar-B-Q.

Feijoada

This is a Brazilian dish that Michael made and won a chili bake off prize for. It's very good. I served it at a dinner party and everyone loved it. I think it's pronounced like Fezwada or close to that. Ask a Brazilian!

2	Cups Dried Black Beans
1	Meaty Soup bone
3/4	Pound Smoked Sausage
1/2	Pound Bacon in one Piece
3/4	Pound Beef Chuck
1	Cup Onion, chopped
3 to 4	Cloves Garlic, minced
2	Cups Canned Tomatoes
1	Can Black Bean Soup
	Salt and Pepper to Taste

- Soak the Beans over Night. In a large pot boil 6 cups of water and add the soaked Beans and Soup bone.
- Bring to a boil and boil for 2 minutes. Turn off the heat and soak for one hour.
- In another pan simmer the Sausage in water for 15 minutes. Drain.
- When cool peel and chop the Sausage. Set aside. Remove the rind from the Bacon. Cut the meat from the Soup Bone. Add both to the Beans and simmer for 1 hour.
- Cut the Chuck into bite size pieces. Add it and the Black Bean soup to the Beans. Simmer for 1 hour.
- Add the cut up Sausage and cook for 30 minutes. Remove the Bacon.

(Continued)

- In a pan melt some Butter and sauté the Onions and Garlic for 5 minutes.
- Add the Tomatoes and cook for another 5 minutes. Add some of the Beans and mash them to make a thick paste. Simmer for 15 minutes. Pour the contents of pan into the beans and simmer for 20 minutes. Always simmer the Beans covered.

This makes about 2 quarts. Serve it with Rice, Orange slices, Sliced Steak and Shrimp in Tomato Sauce for an Authentic Brazilian meal.

It's delicious. It seems lengthy, but it isn't hard and it's worth the effort. Get your ingredients together first and it's fun. It's good with just rice and salad, too.

Zucchini Cheese Puff

Great Side Dish

1	Medium Onion, chopped
1	Pound Zucchini, sliced
5	Eggs
1	Cup Milk
2	Tablespoons Flour
1/4	Teaspoon Salt
1/4	Pound Mushrooms, sliced (About 5 large)
1/2	Pound Mozzarella Cheese, grated
1	Cup (4 ounces) Parmesan cheese or Romano, grated

- Oven 350° for 1 hour
- Combine the Onion and the Zucchini in a cup of water, cover and heat to boiling. Lower the heat and steam for 4 minutes. Drain.
- Beat the eggs with the Milk, Flour, and Salt. Combine with the Zucchini and Onion.
- Add the Mushrooms, Mozzarella, and 1/2 cup Parmesan.
- Turn into greased 1 & 1/2 quart casserole dish.
- Sprinkle with the remaining Cheese.
- Put it in the oven and bake for an hour.

(Continued)

This makes about 6 servings and it's very good alone with a salad or as a side dish with Meat or Chicken.

Chili Relleno Bake

1	Pound Ground Beef
1/2	Cup Onion, chopped
1	Teaspoon Salt, divided
1/4	Teaspoon Pepper
10	Whole Green Chilies, seeded, rinsed, and halved crosswise
4	Eggs, beaten
1 1/2	Cups Milk
1/4	Cup Flour
1 1/2	Cups (6 ounces) Cheddar Cheese, shredded

- Heat the oven to 350°
- Brown the Beef and Onion. Drain the fat. Add 1/2 Teaspoon of the Salt and the Pepper.
- Place half of the Chilies in the bottom of a 12" x 8" Baking Dish. Top with the Meat mixture.
- Arrange the remaining Chilies on top.
- Combine the Eggs, Milk, Flour, and remaining 1/2 Teaspoon Salt. Mix until smooth.

(Continued)

- Pour over the Chilies and top with the Shredded Cheese.
- Bake for 45 minutes or until it's brown and a knife in the middle comes out clean.

This makes a good supper dish and I serve it with black beans and a good salad. Easy too! Serves 6

Stuffed Shells in Jalapeno Sauce

Sauce:

3	Tablespoons Olive Oil
1	Large Onion, chopped
4	Garlic Cloves, minced
1	Jalapeno Pepper, stemmed and minced (I remove the seeds, but be careful as they are so hot. I wear gloves)
1	28 ounce can of Italian tomatoes, crushed, with Juice

- Heat the Oil and add the Onion, Garlic, and Jalapeno. Cover and cook over low heat until onions are soft. Be careful not to burn them.
- Add the tomatoes with juice and bring to a boil. Reduce heat and partially cover. Simmer, stirring occasionally for 30 minutes. Uncover and cook for another 25 minutes on low heat.
- When the sauce is slightly cool, puree it in a food processor. This sauce can be made ahead and refrigerated.

(Continued)

Filling for the Shells:

1	Pound Mild Goat Cheese
8	Ounces of Ricotta at room temperature
1	10 Ounce package Chopped Spinach, thawed and drained and squeezed dry
1/2	Cup Heavy Cream
1	Egg
2	Cups Fresh Basil, minced. (I use the processor)
1/4	Cup Parmesan Cheese
8	Ounces Large Pasta Shells

- Mix the goat cheese and the Ricotta together. Stir in the Spinach, Cream, Egg, Parmesan and Basil.
- Season with Pepper to taste. This can be made ahead and refrigerated.
- Cook the Pasta Shells according to the instructions. The Shells should be firm. Drain and rinse with cold water. Rinse with cold water again.
-
- Preheat the oven to 400°
- Spoon a cup of Sauce in the bottom of a large shallow baking dish.
- Stuff each Shell with a heaping Tablespoon of filling.

(Continued)

- Place the shells filling side up on the Tomato Sauce. Drizzle remaining sauce over Shells.
- Mix 1/4 Cup Parmesan with 2 Tablespoons Bread Crumbs and Sprinkle over the Sauce.
- Bake in the upper part of oven until the mixture is lightly brown and the shells are heated through. About 30 to 40 minutes. Let the Pasta cool for 10 minutes before serving.

If you have any leftover Cheese mixture it's great on bread. Put it under the broiler until it's bubbly.

This is a favorite with everyone and the jalapeno isn't too hot. If you're pushed for time a good canned Tomato Sauce will work.

Poultry, Meat, & Seafood

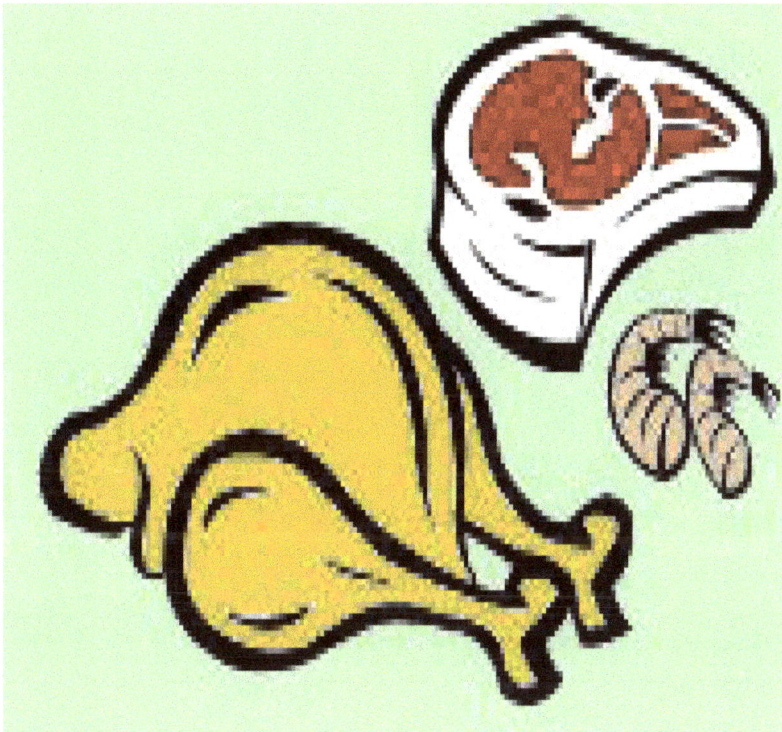

Pacific Paella

4	Chicken Breast Halves, skinned and boned
1	Teaspoon Paprika
1	Teaspoon Salt
1/4	Teaspoon Pepper
1/2	Pound Mild Italian Sausage
1	Can Whole Tomatoes, (14 or 16 ounce can) drained and chopped
2	Cans Chicken Broth
1/2	Teaspoon Turmeric
1/4	Teaspoon Saffron (Optional)
2	Cups Rice
1	Large Onion, cut into wedges
2	Cloves Garlic, minced
1	Pound medium Shrimp, cooked
1	Green Pepper, cut into thin strips
10	Mussels, cleaned and steamed (Optional)

(Continued)

- Cut the Chicken into strips. Combine the Paprika, Salt, and Pepper in a small bowl. Add the Chicken. Stir to coat. Set aside.
- Cut Sausage into 1/4 inch pieces. Remove casing.
- Add enough water to the broth to make 3 3/4 cups. Bring the broth to a boil in 10 inch deep skillet.
- Stir in the Turmeric, Saffron, Rice, Onion, Garlic, Chicken, Sausage, and Tomatoes.
- Reduce the heat and cover tightly. Simmer for 20 minutes.
- Remove from heat and stir in the Shrimp and Green Pepper. Top with the muscles.
- Let stand covered until all the liquid is absorbed. This takes 5 to 10 minutes.

I serve the mussels in a separate bowl as some don't like them. This is another crowd pleaser and easy, too! Serves 10.

Crustless Crab Quiche

2	Teaspoons Olive Oil
1	Medium Red Pepper, chopped
1	Medium Onion, chopped
3/4	Pound Mushrooms, sliced
2	Large Eggs
2	Large Egg Whites
1 1/2	Cups Non-Fat Cottage Cheese
1/2	Cup Non-Fat Plain Yogurt
1/4	Cup All-Purpose Flour
1/4	Cup Parmesan Cheese, grated
1/4	Teaspoon Cayenne Pepper
1/4	Teaspoon Ground Black Pepper
1/2	Pound of Crabmeat (I use the equivalent of lump Crab from a can)
1/2	Cup Low-Fat Cheddar Cheese, grated
1/4	Cup Green Onions, chopped

- Heat the Oven to 350°. Spray a 10 inch pie plate or Quiche dish with cooking spray.

(Continued)

- Heat Oil over medium high heat and add the Onions and Peppers. Cook, stirring until softened, about 5 minutes. Transfer to mixing bowl.
- Add remaining Oil and sauté the Mushrooms until they soften and most of their liquid has evaporated. Add to the Onion mixture.
- In a food processor or blender, blend Eggs, Egg Whites, Cottage Cheese, Yogurt, Flour, Parmesan, Cayenne, Salt, and Pepper until smooth. Mix with Vegetable mix.
- Fold in the Crab, Cheddar, and Green Onions. Pour into prepared dish.
- Bake for 40 to 45 minutes or until a knife inserted in the center comes out clean.
- Let stand 5 minutes before serving. Serves 6.

This is very good and belies the belief that low-fat isn't tasty!

Crab Cakes

Mary Dewitt

2	Pounds Crab Meat (You can use canned if fresh is not available)
2	Egg Yolks, reserve Whites
2	Teaspoons Salt (I use 1 Teaspoon)
1/2	Teaspoon Pepper
1	Teaspoon Dry Mustard
3	Tablespoons Mayonnaise
1	Tablespoon Worcestershire Sauce
2	Tablespoons Chopped Parsley
1	Tablespoon Lemon Juice
2	Cups Soft Bread Crumbs
	Reserved Egg Whites, beaten
2	Tablespoons Butter

- Mix all the ingredients together except the beaten Egg Whites and Butter.
- Fold Egg Whites into Crab mixture. Shape the mix into cakes.
- Melt Butter in large skillet and sauté the Crab Cakes until golden. Turn them gently.

Mary is from Maryland. They know their Crab Cakes! These were a favorite of our Grandson Bryan.

Shrimp Creole
From a Cook in Guayaquil, Ecuador

1/4	Cup Salad Oil
2	Cups Sliced Green Peppers
2	Cups Diced Celery
1	Cup Chopped Celery Leaves
1/2	Cup Chopped Parsley
3 1/2	Tomatoes
1	Cup Chili Sauce
1	Teaspoon Thyme
1	Teaspoon Curry Powder
1	Teaspoon Salt
1	Teaspoon Pepper
1/2	Teaspoon Cayenne
3	Large Bay Leaves
5	Pounds Cleaned Shrimp

- Heat Oil. Add the Onions, Green Pepper, Celery, Celery Leaves. Cook on low heat until the Onions are transparent.
- Add all the rest of the ingredients except the Shrimp. Simmer for 1 hour.
- Add the Shrimp and cook for another hour.
- Serve with Rice, a good Salad, and Crusty Bread. Serves 10.

This is a true favorite of everyone and you can use less Shrimp if you want.

Chicken Breasts Diane

4	Large Boneless Chicken Breast Halves or 8 Small
1/2	Teaspoon Salt
1/2	Teaspoon Pepper
2	Tablespoons Olive Oil
2	Tablespoons Butter
3	Tablespoons Chives or Green Onions, chopped
	Juice of 1/2 Lemon or Lime
2	Tablespoons Cognac or Brandy
3	Tablespoons Parsley, chopped
2	Teaspoons Dijon Style Mustard
1/4	Cup Chicken Broth

- Place the Chicken between plastic wrap and pound slightly with a Mallet. Sprinkle with Salt and Pepper.
- Heat 1 Tablespoon each of Oil and Butter in a large skillet. Do not cook longer as they will be overcooked and dry. Transfer to a warm platter.
- Add the Chive or Onion, Lime Juice, Brandy, Parsley, and Mustard to the pan. Cook for about 15 seconds whisking constantly.
- Whisk in the Broth and stir until the sauce is smooth. Whisk in the remaining Oil and Butter.
- Pour over the Chicken and serve.

It's good with Rice or Noodles.

Crescent Chicken Squares

Filling:

1	3 Ounce Package Cream Cheese, softened
3	Tablespoons Butter, melted
2	Cups Chicken Breasts, cooked and cubed
1/4	Teaspoon Salt
1/4	Teaspoon Pepper
2	Tablespoons Milk
1	Tablespoon Onion, chopped
1	Tablespoon Pimento, chopped
1	6 Ounce Can Crescent Rolls, separated into 4 rectangles

(Continued)

Mix together the first 8 ingredients.

- Spoon 1/2 cup of the Chicken mixture in the center of each rectangle.
- Pull the corners of the dough to the center and press to seal.
- Brush the tops with melted Butter.
- Place on an ungreased baking sheet.
- Bake for 20 to 25 minutes or until golden.

These are easy and delicious. You can double it to make 8. We like them cold, too. Nice for an easy Sunday dinner.

Chicken Wellington

1	Package Puff Pastry
8	Boneless Chicken Breast Cutlets
2	Teaspoon Dried Thyme
	Salt and Pepper
5	Tablespoons Butter
1	Large Onion, finely chopped
1/4	Pound Mushrooms, sliced
2	Tablespoons Parsley, chopped
1	Package Cream Cheese
2	Tablespoons Dijon Mustard
	Egg Wash

- Thaw Pastry for 20 minutes.
- Sprinkle the Chicken with the seasonings.
- In a medium skillet, brown the Chicken in 3 Tablespoons of the Butter. Set the Chicken aside when brown.
- Add the remaining 2 Tablespoons of Butter to the skillet. Sauté the Onions and the Mushrooms until tender and the liquid has evaporated. Stir in the Parsley.

(Continued)

- On a lightly floured surface, roll each sheet into a 14 inch square. Cut each sheet into 4 equal squares.
- Preheat the oven the 375°
- In a small bowl combine the cheese and the mustard. Spread over the Chicken cutlets.
- Spread each square with 2 Tablespoons of the Mushroom mixture. Top with the Chicken Breasts.
- Brush edges of the Pastry with Water and wrap the Pastry around the Chicken, press the edges to seal.
- Place seam side down on an ungreased baking sheet. Brush the top with Egg Wash. (An Egg beaten with 1 Tablespoon of Water)
- Bake for 25 minutes or until puffed and golden brown.

Serves 8

Chicken Florentine

1	Sheet Frozen Puff Pastry
4	Boneless Chicken Breasts
2	Tablespoons Butter
1	Package (10 Ounces) Frozen Spinach, thawed and squeezed dry
1/4	Cup Parmesan Cheese
1/4	Cup Toasted Pine Nuts, chopped
1	Tablespoon Fresh Basil, chopped
1	Small Clove of Garlic, minced
1	Egg Beaten with one Tablespoon of Water (Egg Wash)

(Continued)

- Preheat the oven to 375°
- Thaw the Pastry for 20 minutes.
- Melt the Butter in a skillet. Brown the Chicken Breasts and set aside.
- In a small bowl combine the Spinach, Pine Nuts, Basil, and Garlic.
- Roll the Pastry on a lightly floured surface to a 14 inch square. Cut into four squares.
- Spoon Spinach mixture into the center of each square and top with the Chicken Breasts. Wrap the Pastry to enclose and seal.
- Place seam side down on an ungreased baking sheet. Brush with the Egg Wash and sprinkle with additional Parmesan Cheese.
- Bake 20 minutes or until golden.

You can double this recipe easily to serve 8 for dinner. They're good cold, too.

French Country Chicken

3 to 4 pound whole Chicken
Salt and Thyme
A few sprigs of Parsley
1 whole Onion
6 Red Potatoes
6 small Onions
1/2 cup Sherry

- Preheat the oven to 375°
- Rub the Salt and Thyme in the cavity of the Chicken. Fill the cavity with the sprigs of Parsley and the Onion. Place in a heavy casserole dish and dot with the Butter. Cover and Bake for 30 minutes.
- Meanwhile clean and leave whole 6 small red Potatoes and 6 small Onions.
- Remove the Chicken from the oven and add the prepared Vegetables and the Sherry. Return to the oven and bake for 30 more minutes. Remove the cover at the end of the time and bake until brown and tender. Baste if necessary.

This is a good winter dish and is delicious left over. As you can see the French is the Butter and it does make it taste good.

Baked Chicken Parmesan

2	Frying Chickens cut up. (You can use Boneless Chicken Breasts. It's easier. Just don't cook them as long)
1	Cup Melted Butter
2 to 3	Cloves Crushed Garlic
2 1/2	Tablespoons Dijon Mustard
1 1/2	Teaspoons Worcestershire Sauce
4 1/2	Cups Bread Crumbs (Good way to use old bread)
1 1/4	Parmesan Cheese
1/2	Teaspoon Salt
1/3	Cup Chopped Parsley

- In a large shallow dish combine the melted Butter with the Garlic, Mustard, and Worcestershire Sauce.
- In another dish combine the Bread Crumbs with the Cheese, Salt, and Parsley.
- Dip the Chicken pieces in the melted Butter. Roll in the Crumb mixture, coating well. Place the Chicken in a large baking dish and pour the remaining Butter over all.

(Continued)

- The dish can be made in advance to this point and refrigerated.
- Bake the Chicken pieces for 1 1/2 hours at 350°. If you are using boneless Chicken cut the baking time to half.
- Baste the Chicken with the pan drippings.

I have cut down on the Butter and it's still good. Also I use the Boneless Chicken.

Italian Style Stuffed Chicken

1	Cup Ricotta Cheese
1	Egg
1/2	Cup Parmesan Cheese
1/2	Teaspoon Garlic Salt
2	Packages Frozen Spinach, thawed and well drained.
1	3 to 4 Pound Roasting Chicken
2	Tablespoons Olive Oil
1	Tablespoon Butter
1/4	Teaspoon Rosemary
1/2	Teaspoon Oregano
1/2	Teaspoon Dried Thyme

- Preheat the oven to 350°
- Combine the first 5 ingredients in a small bowl.
- With a sharp knife cut the Chicken completely down the front, splitting the breast bone.
- Press the Chicken down to pop the bones so they lie flat.
- Gently, using your fingers or a boning knife, loosen the skin from the breast portion. Try not to tear the skin. (Do not loosen leg and wing skin))
- Place the Ricotta mixture in the area between the breast and the skin. Press down with your hands to distribute the stuffing evenly.

(Continued)

- Combine the remaining ingredients and Brush it over the entire Chicken.
- Bake for about 1 1/2 hours, brushing occasionally with pan juices. If the stretched skin starts to get too brown cover with foil.
- Cut the Chicken in quarters and serve with pasta and a salad.

This is very good and looks nice, too. It serves 4.

Creamy Chicken Enchiladas

1/2	Pound Boneless, Skinless Chicken Breasts
1/2	Package 10 Ounce Chopped Spinach, Thawed and Drained or 4 Cups Torn Fresh Spinach
1/4	Cup Thinly Sliced Green Onion
1	8 ounce carton Light Sour Cream
1/4	Cup Plain Low Fat Yogurt
2	Tablespoons All Purpose Flour
1/4	Teaspoon Cumin
1/4	Teaspoon Salt
1/2	Cup Skim Milk
1	4 ounce Can Diced Green Chili Peppers, drained
1	7 Inch Flour Tortillas
1/3	Cup Shredded Reduced Fat Cheddar or Monterey Jack Cheese (1 1/2 Ounces)

- Preheat the oven to 350°
- Cook the Chicken in a small amount of water until no longer pink. (You can use leftover Chicken if you have it)
- Remove it from the water and cool. Shred into bite size pieces. You should have about 1 1/2 cups. Set aside.
- Cook the Fresh Spinach if you are using it and drain well.
- In a bowl combine the Chicken, Spinach and Green Onion and set aside.
- In another bowl combine the Sour Cream, Yogurt, Flour, Cumin, and Salt. Divide the Sauce in half. Set one portion aside.

(Continued)

- For the filling combing one portion of the sauce and the Chicken filling mixture.
- Divide the filling among the Tortillas and place seam side down in an ungreased baking dish. At this point the dish can be refrigerated for 24 hours. Store the reserved sauce separately in a covered container. When ready to bake, spoon the reserved Sauce over the Tortillas.
- Bake uncovered about 25 minutes or until heated through. Add 10 to 15 minutes if the dish has been prepared ahead and chilled.
- Sprinkle with Cheese and let stand for 5 minutes. Serve with Salsa, Black Beans, and Avocados.

It's good and light, too. Serves 6

Sour Cream Chicken Enchiladas

Vegetable Oil

12   Corn or Flour Tortillas (I use Corn)

2   Cups cooked Chicken, cut into bite size pieces or Shredded

1   Medium Onion Chopped

1   Pound Monterey Jack and Cheddar mix

- Preheat the oven to 350°
- Combine the Chicken, Onion, and Cheese
- For Corn Tortillas soften in oil heated in a skillet, Drain on paper towel.
- For Flour Tortillas warm in a Microwave of Oven.
- Fill the Tortillas with the Chicken mixture and place seam side down in large baking dish.

Sour Cream Sauce:

1/4 Cup Butter

2   Tablespoons Flour

1   Can or 2 Cups Chicken Broth

1   Cup Light Sour Cream

2   Jalapenos, Seeded and Chopped (Watch those seeds)

- Melt the Butter and whisk in the Flour.
- Remove from heat and whisk in the Broth a little at a time. Stir until smooth.

(Continued)

90

- Return to medium heat and cook until the sauce is thickened and smooth. This is not a very thick sauce, but it's what the dish needs. Whisk in Sour Cream and cook until hot. Do not let it boil or it will curdle. Add the Jalapenos.
- Pour the Sauce over the Enchiladas.
- Bake for 20 minutes.

This is a great recipe, too. We like them both.

Chicken and Artichoke Heart Casserole

3	Packages Frozen Artichoke Hearts
1/2	Cup Butter
1/2	Pound Mushrooms, quartered
6 to 8	Cups Cooked Chicken Breasts, cubed
1/2	Cup Flour
3	Cups Chicken Broth
1	Teaspoon Thyme
	Dash of Nutmeg
4	Cups Cheddar Cheese, grated
1/2	Teaspoon Worcestershire Sauce
	Dash of Tabasco
	Salt and Pepper to Taste
1/2	Cup Bread Crumbs

- Preheat the oven to 350°
- Cook the Artichoke Hearts and place them in the bottom of a 13" x 9" baking dish.
- Sauté the Mushrooms in the Butter until soft. Remove to the baking dish with the Artichokes. Add the Chicken.
- Blend the Flour into the Butter remaining in the pan. Whisk in the Broth slowly and cook until the sauce thickens.
- Add 3 Cups of the Cheese and cook until melted.

(Continued)

- Add the rest of the ingredients except the Bread Crumbs and stir.
- Pour the sauce over the Artichokes, Mushrooms, and Chicken in the baking dish. Top with the Bread Crumbs and the remaining cup of Cheese.
- Bake uncovered for 30 minutes.

This is good with Rice or Noodles. Serves 10.

Rib Eye Roast

Barbara Chelton

1	4 Pound Rib Eye
2	Large Heads Garlic, Crushed
1	Teaspoon Salt
1	Teaspoon Dried Thyme
1	Teaspoon Rosemary
1/2	Teaspoon Coarsely Ground Pepper

- Preheat the oven to 375°
- Rub the Roast with the Salt, Pepper, Garlic, and Herbs.
- Place in a roasting pan and roast to your taste in Beef.

(Continued)

Madera Sauce:

3/4	Cup Madera Wine
1	13 Ounce Can Beef Broth
1	Tablespoon Plus 1 Teaspoon Flour
1	Tablespoon Tomato Paste (The tubes of Tomato Sauce are handy when you need a little and don't want to open a whole can)

- Take the fat from the pan. You can leave a little to blend in the flour. Place the pan on two burners and blend in the flour and the wine. Bring to a boil and boil for 2 to 3 minutes, stirring.
- Add the Broth, Juices from the Roast, and Tomato Paste. Boil, stirring, for 5 minutes.

This is really so good and the Sauce on Mashed Potatoes is the ultimate comfort food. It makes a nice change at Christmas instead of Turkey.

Gypsy Goulash

2	Pounds Lean Beef, cut into strips
3	Tablespoons Olive Oil
6	Onions, thinly sliced
1	Teaspoon Salt
1	Tablespoon Flour
1	Tablespoon Paprika
2	Cups Wine
1	Cup Sour Cream

- Preheat the oven to 375°
- Brown the Meat Strips with the Onions. Blend in the Salt, Flour, and Paprika. Stir to get all the Flour and Seasoning mix into the Meat Strips.
- Add two Cups of Red Wine.
- Turn into an ovenproof casserole dish. Bake covered for 1 1/2 hours. Just before serving add the Sour Cream.

Serve with Noodles and a Crusty Bread for the good sauce. It's an easy tasty dinner for company. In Guatemala, the lean Meat was Lomo Fino, or as they say here, Fillet Mignon. Serves 6 to 8

Mushroom Stuffed Meat Loaf

2	Tablespoons Butter
1	Medium Onion, chopped
1	Pound Mushrooms, diced
1/4	Cup Fresh Parsley, chopped
1/4	Teaspoon Dried Thyme
4	Cups Fresh Bread Crumbs
2	Tablespoons Plus 1/2 Cup Chicken Broth
2	Pounds Ground Beef Chuck
2	Large Eggs
1/2	Cups Ketchup
1/4	Teaspoon Salt
1/8	Teaspoon Pepper

- Preheat the Oven to 375°
- Melt the Butter over medium heat. Add the Onions and cook until golden, stirring occasionally.
- Increase the heat and add the Mushrooms. Cook 5 to 8 minutes longer until the Mushrooms are browned.
- Remove from the skillet and stir in the Parsley, Thyme, 3 cups of the Bread Crumbs, and the 2 Tablespoons of Chicken Broth. Set aside.
- In a large bowl mix the Beef, Eggs, Ketchup, Salt, Pepper, remaining Bread Crumbs, and remaining 1/2 Cup Chicken Broth just until well combined. Do not over mix.

(Continued)

- Press half the Meat mixture into a 9" x 5" Loaf Pan. Top with the Stuffing. Press the remaining Meat mixture into the loaf pan over the stuffing.
- Place the loaf pan on a jelly roll pan to catch any drips during baking.
- Bake Loaf for 1 hour and 30 minutes. Let it stand in the pan for 10 minutes.
- Pour off the fat from loaf pan and invert the loaf onto a platter.

This recipe can be made with leaner ground Beef. I liked the stuffing and it was a little different from plain Meat Loaf. It slices well if you let it stand. Serves 8.

Marinated Pork Tenderloin

Kathleen Sheehy

1/4	Cup soy Sauce
2	Tablespoons Dry Red Wine
1	Tablespoon Honey
1	Tablespoon Brown Sugar
1	Clove Garlic Minced
1/2	Teaspoon Cinnamon Powder
1	Green Onion, Minced
2	Lean Pork Tenderloins

- Mix the first 7 ingredients together. Put in a Ziploc Bag or air tight container and add Pork. Marinate for 2 to 24 hours. The longer the better.
- Remove the Pork and tie together if it's small to prevent the ends from drying out.
- Cook on a grill 40 to 60 minutes depending on size. Baste with the marinade every 15 minutes.
- Slice into thin medallions to serve. You can use Pork Loin instead of Tenderloin if you double the marinade.

This is very good and makes a lovely dinner.

Korean Pork

Pork Tenderloin (These are usually 2 in a package and are about 1 1/2 pounds each)

1/2	Cup soy Sauce
3	Tablespoons Sugar
2	Tablespoons Chopped Onion
2	Cloves Minced Garlic
2	Tablespoons Ginger
3/4	Cup Sesame Seeds
2	Tablespoons Oil

Combine all ingredients. Place the Pork in a large Ziploc Bag. Add the marinade and leave for at least 3 hours. Bake at 325° until tender.

This is a favorite, and it is nice sliced at a buffet. Brings back lots of memories of great parties!

Ribs Supreme

This is the best recipe I know of for Barbecued Ribs.

4	Racks Pork Baby Back Ribs
4	Teaspoons Fresh Ginger, peeled and grated
2	Teaspoons Lemon Zest
3/4	Teaspoon Salt
2	Cloves of Garlic, crushed

- Preheat the oven to 350°.
- In a small bowl mix all the ingredients until combined. Rub the ribs with the mixture until the Ribs are covered.
- Place the Ribs in a large roasting pan overlapping slightly.
- Pour 2 Cups of boiling Water into the roasting pan. Cover tightly with foil. Steam in the oven for 1 hour.
- Carefully remove the foil. Discard the Water. The Ribs may be grilled immediately or refrigerated for up to 2 days.
- Place the Ribs meat side up on a grill over medium heat for 5 minutes, turning once. Brush with Barbecue Sauce. Repeat until browned to your liking.

Braised Lamb Shanks

6 to 8	Lamb Shanks
1	Teaspoon Salt
2	Teaspoons Ground Pepper
1/3	Cup Flour
4	Carrots, cut into 1 1/2 inch quarters
2	Medium Onions, chopped
12	Cloves of Garlic, halved
3/4	Teaspoon Dried Rosemary
2 1/2	Cups Red Wine

- Place the Lamb in a shallow pan. Broil for 15 minutes. Remove from the broiling pan and dust with the Flour. Place in a heavy pot with the other ingredients.
- Bring to a boil. Lower the heat and cook for 1 1/2 to 2 hours. The Lamb should be tender. This is better made ahead.

Reheat in a 300° oven and thicken the sauce if necessary. This is wonderful with Mashed Potatoes. I make it with 2 Lamb Shanks and add all the rest as the sauce is so good.

Baked Goods

Pecan Tassies

From Guayaquil, Ecuador

You need two small muffin tins. These are called Tassie Tins

Crust

1/2	Cup Butter or Margarine at room temperature (I use butter)
1	3 oz package of Cream Cheese at room Temperature
1	Cup of Flour

- Mix the Butter and Cheese with a fork and add the Flour 1/4 cup at a time.
- Refrigerate for an hour.

Filling

1	Egg, beaten with a fork

Add:

3/4	Cup Brown Sugar, packed
2/3	Cup chopped Pecans
1	Tablespoon soft Butter
1/2	Teaspoon Vanilla

Mix together well

- Preheat oven to 350°
- Shape the dough for the crust into Walnut size balls.
- Drop one into each muffin pan, ungreased.
- Shape with your fingers into tart crusts. Make little ridges around the edge.

(Continued)

- Be sure to press the crust firmly to the sides of the little muffin pans!
- Fill with the filling
- Bake for 15 minutes or longer until brown.
- Turn oven down to 250° and bake 10 minutes longer.

It's very important to cool them well in the pans before removing them. Makes 24 Tassies and this recipe can be doubled easily.

Chocolate Chip Cookies

2/3	Cup Shortening
2/3	Cup Butter or Margarine, softened
1	Cup Brown Sugar, packed
1	Cup White Sugar
2	Eggs
2	Teaspoons Vanilla
3	Cups All Purpose Flour
1	Teaspoon Baking Soda
1	Teaspoon Salt
1	Cup Chopped Nuts
12	Ounces Semisweet Chocolate Chips

- Preheat the oven to 375°
- Mix the Shortening, Butter, Sugars, Eggs, and Vanilla thoroughly.
- Stir in the remaining ingredients. (For a softer, rounder cookie add 1/2 cup flour)
- Drop by teaspoonful 2 inches apart on an ungreased cookie sheet.
- Bake 8 to 10 minutes or until lightly browned. Cool slightly before removing from the cookie sheet.

These are an all-time favorite, and I never have tried them with the extra flour.

Brownies

4	Ounces Unsweetened Chocolate
2/3	Cup Shortening
2	Cup Sugar
4	Eggs
1	Teaspoon Vanilla
1 1/4	Cups All-purpose Flour
1	Teaspoon Baking Powder
1	Teaspoon Salt
1	Teaspoon Chopped Nuts

- Melt the Shortening and Chocolate together. Remove from heat and mix in Sugar, Eggs, and Vanilla
- Stir in the remaining ingredients.
- Put the mixture into a 8" or 9" square pan and bake for 30 minutes or until the Brownies start to pull away from the side of the pan. Do not over bake as the Brownies will be dry.
- Cool slightly and cut into bars.

These are good and almost as easy as boxed mix. You can add Chocolate Chips to the mixture before baking. This adds a good Chocolate flavor.

Montego Bay Date Bars

1 1/2	Cup cut up Dates (an 8 oz box of cut up dates is what I use)
2	Tablespoons Sugar
3/4	Cup Water
1/2	Square Unsweetened Chocolate (I use a whole square

- Preheat the oven to 400°
- Cook the Dates, Sugar, Water, and Chocolate over low heat, stirring until the mixture thickens, about 10 minutes.
- Allow the mixture to cool.

1/3	Cup Butter, softened
1/2	Cup Brown Sugar, packed
3/4	Cup All Purpose Flour
1/2	Teaspoon Salt
1/4	Teaspoon Soda
	Grated rind of 1 Orange (This is my addition and is optional)
3/4	Cup Quick cooking Oats
1/3	Cup finely chopped Nuts

(Continued)

- Grease an 8" or 9" square pan
- Cream the Butter and Brown Sugar.
- Mix in the remaining ingredients.
- Press half of the mixture into the bottom of the prepared pan.
- Spread with the cooled Date mixture.
- Top with the remaining Crumb Mixture, press lightly.
- Bake 25 to 30 minutes. Cool and cut into Bars.

Pecan Fingers

3/4	Cup Shortening, softened (Half Butter)
3/4	Cup Confectioner's Sugar
1 1/2	Cups All Purpose Flour

- Preheat the oven to 350°
- Cream the Shortening and Sugar. Blend in the Flour.
- Press evenly into 13' x 9' x 2' pan.
- Bake 12 to 15 minutes.

2	Eggs
1	Cup Brown Sugar
2	Tablespoons Flour
1/2	Teaspoon Baking Powder
1/2	Teaspoon Salt
1/2	Teaspoon Vanilla
1	Cup chopped Pecans

- Mix the ingredients together and .spread over the hot baked layer.
- Bake 20 minutes longer.

Cool and cut into bars. Makes 32 Bars

Gingersnaps

3/4	Cup Shortening
1	Cup Brown Sugar, packed
1	Egg
1/4	Cup Molasses
2 1/4	Cup All Purpose Flour
2	Teaspoons Soda
1	Teaspoon Cinnamon
1	Teaspoon Ginger
1/2	Teaspoon Cloves
1/4	Teaspoon Salt
	Granulated Sugar

- Heat oven to 375°
- Mix the Shortening, Brown Sugar, Eggs, and Molasses thoroughly.
- Blend in the remaining ingredients except the Granulated Sugar and chill for 1 hour.
- Shape the dough by rounded into balls. Place Sugar side up, 3 inches apart on a lightly greased cookie sheet.
- Bake 10 to 12 minutes or until just set. Immediately remove from cookie sheet.

Makes 4 dozen.

Date Bars

1	Cup Chopped Nuts
1	Cup Chopped Dates
1	Cup Powdered Sugar
2	Beaten Eggs
1	Tablespoon Lemon Juice
1	Tablespoon Melted Shortening
1/2	Teaspoon Salt

- Heat oven to 350°
- Combine the Nuts, Dates, Sugar, and Eggs. Mix well.
- Add the other ingredients and mix thoroughly. Pour into greased 9" square pan.
- Bake for 20 to 25 minutes.
- Cut while hot and roll in powdered sugar

Snickerdoodles

With a name like this they have to be good!

1/2	Cup Butter or Margarine
1/2	Cup Shortening
1 1/2	Cups Sugar
2	Eggs
2 3/4	Cups All Purpose Flour
2	Teaspoons Cream of Tartar
1	Teaspoon Soda
1/4	Teaspoon Salt
2	Teaspoons each Sugar and Cinnamon combined

- Preheat the oven to 400°
- Mix the Butter, Shortening, Sugar, and Eggs thoroughly. Blend in the Flour, Cream of Tartar, Soda and Salt. Shape the dough by rounded teaspoons into balls. Roll the balls into the cinnamon sugar mixture.
- Place 2 inches apart on an ungreased cookie sheets.
- Bake for 8 to 10 minutes or until set
- Remove immediately from the sheet.

Makes about 6 dozen.

Russian Teacakes

Also called Mexican wedding cakes. They always appear at Christmas, but they are great all year round. Delicious and easy.

1	Cup Butter or Margarine (They are better with Butter)
1/2	Cup Confectioner's Sugar
1	Teaspoon Vanilla
2 1/4	Cups All Purpose Flour
1/4	Teaspoon Salt
3/4	Cup Finely Chopped Nuts. Use the food processor.

- Heat the oven to 400°
- Mix the butter, sugar, and vanilla thoroughly. Work in the flour, salt, and nuts until the dough holds together.
- Shape into 1 inch balls. Place on an ungreased cookie sheet
- Bake 10 to 12 minutes or until set. Do not brown.
- While they're warm roll them in confectioner's sugar. Cool. Roll in sugar again.

Makes about 4 dozen.

Apricot Kolaches

1	Cup 12 oz. Jar Apricot Preserves (about 1 cup)
1/2	Cup Finely Chopped Walnuts or Pecans
1/4	Teaspoon Ground Cinnamon
1/4	Teaspoon Ground Nutmeg
1/4	Teaspoon Ground Cloves
1	Cup Butter or Margarine, softened
1	8 oz Package Cream Cheese, softened
2	Tablespoons Sugar
2	Cups All Purpose Flour
1	Large Egg, lightly beaten
1	Tablespoon Water
	Sifted Powdered Sugar

- Heat oven to 350°
- Combine the first five ingredients and set aside.
- Beat the Butter and Cream Cheese at medium speed with an electric mixer until creamy.
- Add the Sugar, beating well.

(Continued)

- Add the flour, mixing at low speed until well blended.
- Divide the dough into thirds. Roll each portion to 1/8" thickness on a floured board.
- Cut into 3" rounds with a cookie cutter.
- Spoon 1/2 teaspoon of the Apricot Filling into the center of each round.
- Combine the egg and water. Brush it on edges of rounds.
- Fold opposite sides to center slightly overlapping edges and pinch to seal. Two ends will be open.
- Bake for 12 minutes or until golden
- Remove to a wire racks to cool and sprinkle with powdered sugar.

Seven Layer Bars

1/2	Cup Butter
1	Cup Graham Cracker Crumbs
1	Cup Coconut
6	Ounces Semi-sweet Chocolate Chips
6	Ounces Butterscotch Chips or Toffee Bits
1	15 oz Can Eagle Brand Milk
1	Cup Chopped Nuts

- Preheat the oven to 350°
- Melt the Butter in a 13" x 9" x 2" baking dish. Sprinkle with the Crumbs and then sprinkle the other ingredients except for the Milk and Nuts over the crumb mixture.
- Pour the milk over all. Sprinkle the nuts on top and press lightly.
- Bake for 30 minutes.
- Cool in the pan and cut into squares.

It makes about 40 squares. The edges are usually quite brown and may have to be discarded.

Coconut Butterscotch Squares

3/4	Cup Flour
1/2	Teaspoon Baking Powder
1/2	Teaspoon Salt
1/4	Cup Soft Shortening
1	Cup Packed Brown Sugar
1	Egg
1	Teaspoon Vanilla
1	Cup Coconut
1	Teaspoon Melted Butter
1	Tablespoon Sugar
1/2	Cup Coconut

(Continued)

- Heat the oven to 350°
- Grease an 8" x 8" x 2" pan
- Mix together the Flour, Baking Powder, and Salt. Set aside.
- Mix the Shortening, Brown Sugar, Egg, and Vanilla until very fluffy. Mix in the Flour mixture and the cup of Coconut.
- Put into the prepared pan.
- Mix the remaining ingredients together. Sprinkle over the Batter in the pan.
- Bake for 30 to 35 minutes.
- Cut into squares while warm. Cool in the pan.

I got this recipe from someone I met in Saudi Arabia. Makes 16 squares.

Stir-N-Drop Sugar Cookies

Guayaquil – 1974

2	Eggs
2/3	Cups Vegetable Oil
2	Teaspoons Vanilla Extract
1	Teaspoon Almond Extract
3/4	Cup Sugar
2	Cups Flour
2	Teaspoons Baking Powder
1/2	Teaspoon Salt

- Preheat the oven to 400°
- Beat the Eggs with a fork until well blended. Stir in the Oil, Vanilla Extract, and Almond Extract. Blend in the Sugar.
- Mix the Flour, Baking Powder, and Salt. Blend into the oil mixture.
- Drop by teaspoons 2" apart on an ungreased cookie sheet. Gently press each cookie with the bottom of a glass that has been dipped in sugar.
- Bake 8 to 10 minutes. Remove from sheet immediately when baked.

These are good and easy.

Nut Toffee

Hilton Head, SC

1	Pound Nuts (1/3 Walnuts, 1/3 Almonds, 1/3 Pecans
1	Pound Melting Milk Chocolate
2	Sticks Butter
2	Sticks Margarine
2	Cups Sugar

It will go much easier if you have everything ready before starting the toffee.

- Finely chop the nuts. Use the steel blade in the food processor.
- Line two cookie sheets with sides (10" x 15") with aluminum foil. Anchor it over the ends of the pans.
- Spray the pans with cooking spray.
- Cover two pieces of news paper with wax paper so they are ready when needed.
- Using a 3 quart heavy saucepan, melt the Butter. Add the sugar and half the nuts.
- Boil hard on medium heat, stirring constantly with a wooden spoon until the temperature on a candy thermometer reaches 300°. The end product is better if you get it to 300° or beyond. But be careful. It burns easily at this point!
- Remove from heat and pour into the prepared cookie sheets.
- Spread with a spatula that has been sprayed with cooking spray.

(Continued)

- Melt the Chocolate in a large measuring cup in the microwave.
- Spread 1/4 of Chocolate over the Toffee in each pan. Sprinkle with 1/4 of the remaining nuts.
- Place the wax paper on top and then the newspaper. Flip the cookie sheet quickly.
- Remove the wax paper and spread with 1/2 the remaining Chocolate and 1/2 the remaining nuts. Repeat with the other pan.

It is better to work with both pans before doing the Chocolate as they will both be warm. I use all Butter, but the recipe called for Margarine.

- Allow the candy to cool in the refrigerator and then break it into pieces and store it in a tight tin in the freezer.

It is a nice Christmas gift packed in a pretty tin or box. Besides that, it is delicious.

Blender Banana Bread

Anita Emmons

- Oven 350°
- Grease and flour loaf pan.
- Sift together and set aside:

2	Cups Flour
1 1/2	Teaspoons Baking Powdcr
1/2	Teaspoons Salt
1/2	Teaspoon Soda
1/4	Teaspoon Nutmeg

(Continued)

- In a blender mix until smooth:

1/2	Cup Soft Butter
2	Eggs
1	Cup Sugar
3	Tablespoons Sour Cream
1	Tablespoon Lemon Juice

- Add 1 1/2 Cups sliced Bananas and blend. Add 1/2 Cup Pecans and blend only until broken.
- Mix the liquid mixture into the flour mixture until well combined. Pour into prepared pan and bake for 50 minutes. Cool a bit, and remove from it from the pan.

I slice it when it's cold and freeze some. It's delicious for breakfast.

Date Nut Bread

1	Package (8 ounces) Chopped Pitted Dates
3/4	Cup Boiling Water
1/4	Cup Orange Juice
3	Cups All Purpose Flour
1/2	Teaspoon Salt
1	Teaspoon Baking Soda
1	Cup Sugar
1/2	Cup Butter or Margarine
2	Eggs
1/2	Cup Sour Cream
1	Teaspoon Grated Orange Peel
1	Cup Chopped Nuts

- Preheat oven to 350° and grease and flour two 8 1/2" x 4 1/2" loaf pans.
- Combine the Dates, Water, and Orange Juice. Set aside to cool.
- Stir together the Flour, Salt, and Soda. Set aside.
- Cream the Sugar and Butter together.

(Continued)

- Add the Eggs, Sour Cream, Orange Peel, and cooled Date mixture. Mix until blended.
- Stir in the Flour mixture until just moistened.
- Fold in the chopped Nuts.
- Pour into prepared pans and bake 50 to 60 minutes or until a cake tester in the center comes out clean.
- Cool 10 minutes in the pans. Remove to wire rack to complete cooling. Wrap tightly and store in the refrigerator.

Sweet Rolls

Dough

2	Packages Active Dry Yeast
1/2	Cup Warm Water (105° to 115°)
1/2	Cup Luke Warm Milk
1/2	Cup Sugar
1	Teaspoon Salt
2	Eggs
1/2	Cup Shortening, Soft Butter or Margarine
4 1/2	Cups Flour (5 cups if needed)

- Dissolve the Yeast in the Water.
- Stir in the Milk, Sugar, Salt, Eggs, Shortening and 2 1/2 Cups of the Flour. Beat until smooth.
- Mix in the remaining Flour to make the dough easy to handle. Turn the dough out onto a floured board. Knead until smooth and elastic, about 5 minutes. Add a bit more flour if it's too sticky.
- Put it in a greased bowl. Turn greased side up. (At this point you can refrigerate the dough for 3 to 4 days)
- Cover and let it rise in a warm place until doubled, about 1 1/2 hours.

(Continued)

- The dough is ready if an impression remains when it's touched. Mommy Sheehy said when you stuck your finger in it and the hole stayed there!
- While the dough is rising mix together 1/2 Cup Sugar and 6 Teaspoons Cinnamon. Measure 4 Tablespoons of softened butter. This is enough for both portions of the dough.
- Punch down the dough when it's ready. Cut the dough into 2 portions. Roll each portion into a rectangle. Spread each one with 2 tablespoons of Butter.
- Sprinkle half the Cinnamon mix on the each rectangle. Roll up beginning at the wide side. Pinch the edge of the dough to seal.
- Cut the roll into about 15 slices. Sometimes you get less.
- Place the slices slightly apart in a greased 13" x 9" x 2" baking dish. Repeat with the other half of the dough.
- Bake in a preheated 375° oven for 25 to 30 minutes. Check them as you don't want them to get too brown.

For Cinnamon Rolls with Butterscotch-Pecan or Walnut topping:

- Before rolling the dough into a rectangle, melt 1/4 cup of Butter or Margarine in each baking pan. Stir in 1/2 cup Pecans or Walnut halves. I use chopped nuts too. Spread in the pan.
- Roll and slice the dough and bake as directed. Immediately turn the pan upside down on a large tray.
- Let the pan remain a minute or two so the Butterscotch dribbles over the rolls.

(Continued)

When we lived in Guatemala these were always made for Christmas breakfast and at Easter to take to San Luis. Later when the family came to visit we had them at big breakfast. John loved them. I don't make them much anymore, but they sure beat the ready-mades!

When making bread it is best if you remember to have the eggs at room temperature and if using Butter to have it soft. Make sure your yeast is fresh. (A little bit of sugar in the water with the yeast will show a slight movement of the mix) Water that is too hot will kill the yeast. Water that is too cool will merely slow down the rising.

Add the second amount of flour slowly so you don't add too much. Also for rolls the dough is softer than regular bread. A few tips from the pros as bread is fun to make, smells heavenly baking, and is great to eat. It is a feel good baking project.

Golden Crescents

2	Packages Dry Yeast
3/4	Cup Warm Water (105° to 115°)
1/2	Cup Sugar
1	Teaspoon Salt
2	Eggs
1/2	Cup shortening (Part Soft butter)
4	Cups Flour
	Soft Butter or Margarine

- Dissolve the yeast in warm water. Stir in Sugar, Salt, Eggs, Shortening and 2 cups Flour. Beat until smooth.
- Mix in the remaining flour until smooth. Scrape the dough from the sides of the Bowl.
- Cover and let rise in a warm place until double, about 1 1/2 hours.
- Divide the dough in half. Roll each wedge beginning at the round edge.
- Cover and let it rise until double, about 1 hour.
- Heat the oven to 400°. Bake 12 to 15 minutes or until golden brown.

Yogurt Crescent Rolls

These have half the fat!

1/3	Cup Vegetable Oil
1	8 oz carton plain low fat yogurt
1/2	Cup Sugar
2	Packages Dry Yeast
1/2	Cup Warm Water (105° - 115°)
1	Egg
1	Egg White
4	Cups All Purpose Flour
1	Teaspoon Salt
	Butter Flavored Cooking Spray

- Combine the first 3 ingredients. Set aside.
- Dissolve the Yeast in Warm Water in a large mixing Bowl. Let stand for 5 minutes.
- Stir in the Yogurt mixture, Egg, and Egg White. Combine the Flour and Salt.
- Stir 2 Cups of the Flour into the Yogurt Mixture. Beat at medium speed until smooth. Gradually stir in the remaining Flour.
- Cover and refrigerate for 8 hours.

(Continue)

- Punch the dough down, and divide it into 4 equal parts. Roll each part into a 10 inch circle on a floured surface.
- Cut each circle into 12 wedges. Roll up beginning at the wide end.
- Coat a baking sheet with cooking spray and place the crescents point side down.
- Cover and let rise in a warm place free from drafts for 45 minutes or until doubled in size.
- Bake in preheated 375° oven for 10 to 12 minutes or until golden. It makes 4 dozen.

Approximate Nutritional Information

Calories 66
Fat 1.9 gr
Cholesterol 5 mg
They taste good, too!

Cakes And Pies

Almond Streusel Cake

Streusel

1	Cup Firmly Packed Light Brown Sugar
1	Cup Sliced Almonds
1	Cup All Purpose Flour
3	Tablespoons Butter, melted
1	Teaspoon Grated Orange Zest

Cake

1/2	Cup (1 stick) Butter, melted
1/2	Cup Sugar
3	Large Eggs
1	Teaspoon Grated Orange Zest
1/2	Teaspoon Vanilla Extract
2	Cups All Purpose Flour
1	Teaspoon Baking Powder
1	Teaspoon Baking Soda
1/3	Cup Orange Juice

Glaze

1/2	Cup Confectioner's Sugar
2-1/2	Teaspoons Orange Juice

(Continued)

- Preheat the Oven to 350° Grease a 9" or 10" tube pan.
- **Streusel**: in a medium bowl, stir together the Brown Sugar, Nuts, and Flour. Stir in the Butter and Zest.
- **Cake:** in a large bowl, beat together on medium speed, the Butter and Sugar until fluffy. Add the Eggs one at a time. Beat in the Zest and Vanilla.
- In a large bowl, mix together the Flour, Baking Powder, and Baking Soda.
- Reduce mixer speed to low. Alternately beat the Flour mixture and Orange Juice into the Egg mixture beginning and ending with the Flour.
- Spoon half of the batter into the prepared pan. Sprinkle with half of the streusel. Top with the remaining batter and streusel.
- Bake 30 to 35 minutes. Test with a tooth pick. Transfer the pan to a wire rack to cool completely.
- **Glaze:** stir together the Confectioners' Sugar and Orange Juice until smooth.
- Turn the cake out onto a serving plate, placing it right side up. Drizzle with the glaze.

Cocoa Pink Cupcakes

2	Cups Flour
1	Tablespoon Cocoa
1	Teaspoon Salt
2/3	Cup Shortening
1-1/2	Cups Sugar
1	Egg
1	Teaspoon Vanilla
1	Teaspoon Baking Soda
1	Cup Cold Water
	Chocolate Chips
	Pecan or Walnut Pieces

- Preheat the oven to 375° Put paper cup liners in the Muffin Tin.
- Sift the Flour, Cocoa and Salt together twice. Set aside.
- Cream the Shortening and gradually add the Sugar. Add the Egg and Vanilla. Mix well.
- Combine the Water and Soda in a separate bowl. Alternately add the dry mixture and the water mixture to the creamed sugar. Starting and ending with the dry mixture.
- Fill the muffin cups 1/2 full and sprinkle generously with the chips and nuts.
- Bake 20 to 25 minutes.
- Makes about 12 muffins.

This is a favorite with everyone.

Gingerbread Cake Roll

Oil the bottom and sides of a 15"x10"x 1" Jelly Roll Pan. Line the pan with wax paper. Oil and flour the paper. Set aside.

Preheat oven to 350°

3	Eggs Separated
1	Tablespoon Butter Melted
1/3	Cup Molasses
1/4	Cup Sugar
1	Cup Flour
3/4	Teaspoon Baking Powder
3/4	Teaspoon Baking Soda
1/8	Teaspoon Salt
1/2	Teaspoon Ground Cinnamon
1/2	Teaspoon Ground Cloves
1/2	Teaspoon Ground Ginger

- Mix the flour and next 6 ingredients. Set aside. Beat Egg Whites until foamy (Egg whites are better when at room temperature)
- Gradually add the sugar, beating until stiff but not dry. Fold the whites into the egg yolk mixture. Gradually fold the flour mixture into the egg mixture.

(Continued)

137

- Spread the batter into the prepared Pan. Bake for 8 to 10 minutes.
- Sift the powdered sugar on a cloth towel the size of the pan.
- When the cake is done, immediately loosen it from the sides of the pan and turn it out onto the sugared cloth. Peel off the wax paper.
- Starting from the narrow end, roll the cake and cloth together. Cool completely on a wire rack seam side down.
- While the cake is cooling make the spiced cream.

1 1/2	Cups Whipping Cream
1/3	Cup Powdered Sugar
1	Teaspoon Ground Cinnamon
1/4	Teaspoon Ground Cloves
1	Teaspoon Vanilla

- When cake is cooled unroll and spread with 1/2 of the Spiced Cream.
- Carefully reroll
- Place on cake plate seam side down
- Spread with remaining cream.
- Pull an icing comb or fork along the top if you want for decoration.

This makes 8 to 10 servings and is especially good at Thanksgiving or Christmas.

Applesauce Cake with Burnt Sugar Sauce

4	Cups Apples, diced
2	Cups Flour
2	Teaspoons Baking Soda
1	Teaspoon Nutmeg
1	Teaspoon Cinnamon
1/2	Teaspoon Salt
1	Cup Chopped Walnuts
1	Cup Butter
2	Cups Sugar
2	Eggs Beaten

- Preheat the oven to 350°
- Grease a 13"x 9"baking pan.
- Cream the Butter, Sugar and Eggs
- Mix the dry ingredients together. Add the Apples and Nuts.
- Add the dry ingredients to the creamed mixture and mix well.
- Pour it into the prepared pan.
- Bake 45 minutes.

(Continued)

Sauce

1	Cup Butter
1	Cup Sugar
1	Cup Brown Sugar Packed
1	Cup Half-n-Half

- Mix together and boil for about 2 minutes.
- Serve over cake and top with Vanilla Ice Cream or Whipped Cream.

This is not for the diet conscious but it's delicious served in small portions. Comfort Food!

Fruitcake

Type of pan:

1	10" tube pan (Recipe Doubled)	Bake for 3 ¼ hours
1	8"x 2 ½" loaf pan	Bake for 2 ½ hours
6	4 ½" x 2 ½" individual loaf pans	Bake for 1 ½ hours

- Line the pans with greased brown paper. The pans can be filled within 1/2 inch of the top.

This is the Master Recipe and can be doubled with no problem. To double it, make a separate batch.

1	1 pound Jar Mixed Candied Fruit
1	Cup each: Light Raisins, Dark Raisins, and coarsely chopped Walnuts.
1/2	Cup each coarsely chopped Almonds and Flour

- Toss together in a zip lock bag or big bowl and set aside.

(Continued)

141

1/2	Cup Sugar
1/2	Cup Brown Sugar Packed
1/4	Cup Butter Softened
3	Eggs
1/4	Cup Brandy or almost any Spirit or Fruit Juice, Wine or Strong Coffee.
1/4	Cup Applesauce
1/2	Teaspoon Almond Extract
1	Cup (more) Flour sifted with 1/4 Teaspoon each Allspice, Cinnamon, and Baking Soda.

- In a large bowl combine sugars and butter. Beat until light and fluffy.
- Add the Eggs and beat 2 minutes longer.
- Stir in the Brandy, applesauce, and almond Extract.
- Gradually add the Flour mixture. Beat only until dampened.
- Turn the Fruit and Nut mixture into the batter. Mix well with a large spoon.
- Spoon the batter into the prepared pans and bake according to directions above or until a cake tester comes out clean when inserted in the middle.
- Cool on a rack, remove the paper, and wrap well after you have dribbled with the Spirit of your choice.

This is a delicious cake and those who like fruitcake really like it. Those who don't like fruitcake, more for us!

We used to make lots of these to sell at the women's club Christmas Bazaar when we lived in Guayaquil, Ecuador. They were a big hit!

Mocha Fudge Pie

This is a big hit with chocolate lovers and truly is not fattening. Save the other half of the brownie mix for another pie.

Crust:

1/3	Cup Hot Water
2	Teaspoons Instant Coffee Granules
1/2	Box Light Fudge Brownie Mix (about 2 cups)
1	Teaspoon Vanilla

* Preheat the oven to 325°
* Coat a 9" pie plate with cooking spray.
* Combine the hot water and 2 Teaspoons Coffee in a medium bowl. Stir well.
* Add the Brownie mix, Vanilla, and Egg Whites. Stir until well blended. Pour into pie plate.
* Bake 22 Minutes. Cool completely.

(Continued)

Filling:

3/4	Cup Low Fat Milk
3	Tablespoons Coffee flavor liqueur.
2	Teaspoons instant Coffee.
1	Teaspoon Vanilla
1	3.9 ounce Chocolate Instant Pudding and Pie mix
3	Cups Frozen Reduced Calorie Whipped Topping, thawed and divided

- Combine the Milk, 2 Tablespoons of the Coffee flavored liqueur, 1 Teaspoon of the Coffee, the Vanilla, and the Pudding Mix. Beat at medium speed for 1 minute.
- Gently fold in 1 1/2 cups of the Whipped Topping. Spread the mixture evenly over cooled Brownie Crust.
- Combine the remaining Liqueur and Coffee in a bowl. Stir well. Gently fold in the remaining topping. Spread evenly over Pudding mixture and Garnish with Chocolate Curls.

Serve immediately or chill. 8-10 servings.

Strawberry Pie

Milly Williams in Hilton Head

Preheat Oven to 400°

Crust:

1-1/2	Cup Flour
1/2	Teaspoon Salt
1/2	Cup Oil
2	Teaspoons Milk

- Stir together all ingredients with a fork and Press into a 10" pie plate.

"This is a shiny greasy mess but have faith," A quote from Milly.

Filling:

1	Cup Sugar
1	Tablespoon Lemon Juice
1	Cup Smashed Strawberries
1	Teaspoon Almond Extract
2	Egg Whites

- In large bowl in mixer beat the egg whites into soft peaks.

  Add remaining ingredients.

(Continued)

- Beat 15 to 20 minutes. It will really grow.
- Fold in 1 cup of Heavy Whipped Cream.
- Add sliced Berries if desired.
- Put in Pie Crust and Refrigerate until ready to serve.

Delicious, light, and easy
Serves 8 to 10 depending on slice size.

Berry Cream Tart

For the Crust:

1/2	Cup Finely Chopped Pecans
2 1/2	Tablespoons Sugar
1/2	Stick Butter Melted and Cooled

For the Filling:

8	Ounces Cream Cheese, softened
1/2	Cup Confectioner's Sugar
1	Teaspoon Vanilla
1	Tablespoon Grand Marnier
1	Cup of Well Chilled Heavy Cream
4	Cups of Assorted Berries or you can use all the same

(Continued)

- Make crust in a food processor. Blend crumbs, pecans, sugar, and butter for 10 seconds (Mixture will resemble fine meal)
- Transfer mixture to buttered fluted 11 inch pan with removable bottom.
- Press into sides and bottom of pan.
- Bake in a preheated over for 2 to 10 minutes or until golden.
- Let Crust cool completely in the pan.
- In food processor blend Cheese, Sugar, Vanilla, and Grand Marnier.
- In a chilled bowl, beat cream until it holds stiff peaks. Whisk the Cheese mixture gently into Whipped Cream and spoon onto cooled crust.
- Arrange Berries decoratively on top, cover loosely, and chill until serving.
- Remove sides of pan and serve.

Makes 8 to 10 servings with rave reviews!

Sunshine Pie

1	4 ounce package Lemon Pudding and Pie Mix
1/2	Cup Sugar
1 3/4	Cups Water, divided
1	Egg Slightly Beaten
1 1/2	Cups of Whipped Topping
1/2	Cup Shredded Sweetened Coconut
1	Prepared Graham Cracker Crust (I use the crust from the Berry and Cream Tart as it is very good with this pie. You can put it into a 9" pie pan and bake the same way)

- If using your own crust, prepare, bake, and allow to cool.
- In a medium sauce pan beat together Pudding, Sugar, 1/4 Cup Water, and Egg. When well blended add remaining water and blend well.
- Cook over medium heat stirring until mixture boils, about 5 minutes
- Remove from heat. Cool to room temperature stirring occasionally.
- When cooled whisk lightly and fold in the Whipped Topping and Coconut until evenly mixed.
- Spoon into crust and refrigerate until set about 40 minutes.

This is an excellent easy lemon pie. Browned Coconut on top is nice.

Beach Plum's Bombe Favorite with Raspberry Sauce

10 to 12 Servings

Meringue Filling

5	Egg Whites, at room temperature
1 1/2	Cups Granulated Sugar
2	Cups Heavy Cream
2	Tablespoons Confectioners' Sugar
2	Tablespoons Kirsch or Rum
1/2	Teaspoons Vanilla Extract

Sauce

2	Packages (10 Ounces each) Frozen Raspberries, Thawed
1/4	Cup Confectioners' Sugar, Sifted
1	Tablespoon Kirsch or Rum

(Continued

- Prepare the filling: Preheat the Oven to 250°. Line 2 large cookie sheets with parchment or brown paper. Trace 4 circles 4 inches in diameter on one sheet and 5 circles the same size on the other.
- Beat the Egg Whites until soft peaks form. Gradually beat in the Granulated Sugar, about 2 tablespoons at a time. Continue beating until stiff peaks form. Spoon or pipe the misture onto the sheets to fill the circles. (The meringues are broken into small pieces later, so don't worry if your circles are not perfect.
- Bake the meringues until lightly browned and crisp to the touch, about 1 hour.
- Transfer them on the paper to a wire rack and let cool completely. Peel off the paper. Break the m eringues into 1/4 inch pieces and place in a large bowl. (If making them ahead, keep the meringues whole and store in an airtight tin.)
- Beat the cream until soft peaks form. Beat in the Confectioners' Sugar, Kirsch, and Vanilla. Combine the cream with the broken meringue pieces and gently fold to mix.
- Spoon into a lightly oiled 8" springform pan, smooth the top. Cover with foil and freeze until firm, 6 hours or overnight.

(Continued)

- Make the Sauce: Drain the Raspberries, reserving 1 cup of the syrup. Puree them in a blender or food processor. Pass through a fine strainer to remove the seeds. You should have about 1/2 cup of puree. Stir in the reserved syrup.
- Place the Raspberry puree in a small saucepan over low heat and gradually whisk in the Sugar. Cook until the mixture thickens slightly, about 1 minute. Remove from the heat. Let cool for 5 minutes. Stir in the Kirsch, cover and refrigerate until chilled.
- To serve, loosen the edges of the bombe with a sharp knife, release the side of the springform pan. Cut the bombe into wedges and spoon about 2 tablespoons of sauce over each portion. Pass the remaining sauce in a small bowl.

Meringues need dry weather. Turn off the oven and leave them until you need them. You can use any sauce.

Pumpkin Pie Cake

2	15 Ounce Cans Pumpkin
1	Cup Sugar
1	12 Ounce Can Evaporated Milk
3	Eggs
1/4	Teaspoon Each Nutmeg, Cloves, Allspice
1	Teaspoon Cinnamon
1	Yellow Cake Mix
1	Stick Butter or Margarine, Melted

(Continued)

- Combine Pumpkin, Sugar, Milk, Eggs, and Spices until well combined.
- Pour into a 9" x 13" pan sprayed with cooking spray.
- Sprinkle dry cake mix over mixture. (Don't mix)
- Drizzle with melted Butter.
- Bake for 45 minutes at 375°.

Enjoy!

Desserts

Lemon Ambrosia Dessert

Mary Marston
Hilton Head

6	Eggs, separated
3/4	Cup of Sugar
	Juice and grated Rind of 2 Large Lemons
1	Small Package of Lemon Jello
1	Scant Cup of Boiling Water
3/4	Cup Sugar (This is for the Egg Whites)
2	Packages of Plain Ladyfingers
1/2	Cup Heavy Cream
1/2	Teaspoon Vanilla

- Prepare an 8" Spring Form Pan by lining bottom and sides with Ladyfingers.
- Put the Egg Yolks in a double boiler mixed with Sugar, Lemon Juice, and Rind.
- Cook until thick, stirring constantly.
- Dissolve Jello in Boiling Water. Cool and add to the Egg Yolk mixture.
- Beat Egg Whites until stiff gradually adding the 3/4 cup of Sugar.
- Fold into Yolk mixture and pour into the prepared pan.
- Refrigerate overnight.
- Cover the top with whipped cream and toasted coconut if desired.

(Continued)

It is very nice served with puree of Raspberries:

- Thaw frozen berries. Using processor, puree them and strain out seeds. Add desired amount of Sugar and serve with slice of Ambrosia.

This will serve 12 easily. Easy to prepare and can be made ahead.

Chocolate Lady Finger Dessert

Mary Marston in Hilton Head

2-1/2	Packages of Plain Lady Fingers
8	Ounces Semisweet Chocolate
4	Tablespoons of Boiling Water
6	Eggs, Separated
3	Tablespoons of Powdered Sugar
2	Teaspoons of Vanilla

- Line a loaf pan with wax paper and then Lady Fingers.
- Melt Chocolate with Boiling Water in top of Double Boiler. Cool slightly and beat in Egg Yolks one at a time. Add Sugar and Vanilla and Mix.
- Beat Egg Whites and Fold into the Chocolate Mixture.
- Pour some into the prepared pan and cover with Ladyfingers. Continue alternating Chocolate and Ladyfingers ending with Ladyfingers on top.
- Cover with wax paper and refrigerate overnight.
- When ready to serve cover with whipped cream and Dribble with melted Chocolate. Cut in slices.

They are very pretty with the Chocolate and the White Ladyfingers. Serves 10 to 12.

Chocolate-Cinnamon Torte

Make the cookies several days ahead.

2 3/4	Cups Flour
2	Tablespoons Cinnamon
1 1/2	Cups Butter, softened
2	Cups Sugar
2	Eggs, beaten

- Preheat the oven to 375°. Draw a 9" circle on each of two 12" pieces of wax paper.
- Place each piece on greased cookie sheet.
- Sift Flour with cinnamon and set aside
- In a large bowl with the mixer at medium speed, mix the Butter with the Sugar. Then mix in the Eggs until very light and fluffy.
- With mixer at low speed, mix in the Flour a little at a time until smooth.
- With small spatula spread 1/3 cup of the Cookie dough in a very thin layer on each circle of Wax Paper.
- Bake in oven on 2 racks 8 to 10 minutes or until golden.
- Invert on cake racks. Peel off the wax paper and cool.
- Continue baking cookies in thes manner until the dough is used up. Make at least 12. Store carefully stacked in a tight container.

(Continued)

Filling:

1	Square Unsweetened Chocolate
2	Squares Semisweet Chocolate
4	Cups Heavy Cream
2	Tablespoons Cocoa
12	Glazed Cherries
12	Walnut Halves

- Grate the Unsweetened Chocolate Medium Fine.
- With Vegetable peeler shred Semisweet chocolate into Curles.
- Whip the Cream.
- On a cake plate spread a little Whipped Cream. Place one cookie on top. Spread it with 1/4 to 1/3 cup Whipped Cream.
- Continue building layers this way until you have a 12 Layer Torte.
- Fold the Unsweetened Chocolate into leftover Whipped Cream. Heap this on top of the Torte.
- Decorate with the Cherries Walnuts and Chocolate Curls.
- Refrigerate for at Least 1/2 hour before serving so it can be easily cut into 16 wedges.

This is easy if you make the cookies ahead. You can flavor the Whipped Cream if you want. It is impressive and Delicious. Don't worry if a cookie breaks. No one will know.

Mocha Ice Cream

Kay Marachulio – Guatemala

Prepare 12 Muffin Tins with Paper Cups.
Boil for three minutes:

1/2	Cup Sugar
1/2	Water
1 1/2	Teaspoon Instant Coffee

- Put 6 ounces Chocolate Chips into a blender and Add the Sugar Mixture and Blend.
- Add 2 Eggs (You can use only whites if you want). Blend.
- Pour into a bowl and fold in 1 1/2 cups Whipped Cream.
- Put the same amount of the mixture into each paper cup and Freeze until ready to use.

You can take them out of the tins and store in a zip lock bag in the freezer. They defrost quickly and are very good with sliced strawberries and a little additional Whipped Cream. A delicious and easy desert.

Crème Caramel

Merci Armador – Saudi Arabia

This is a very easy recipe for a delicious Flan.

Preheat Oven to 350°.

First Prepare the Caramel.

1	Cup of Water
1	Cup of Sugar

- Measure into a good size pot.
- Cook until it is a nice caramel color. This takes a few minutes and it's better to do it slowly than to burn it.
- Remove from heat and pour into a prepared pan. I use a 4 cup ring mold. Merci used a Danish Cookie Can.
- Mix 1 can of condensed milk with 1 can measure of plain milk. Strain 4 Eggs to remove the white bits. They don't look nice when the Flan is served.
- Pour the Milk Egg mixture into the pan with the Caramel.
- Put the pan into a baking pan with boiling water and bake for 1 hour or until a knife comes out clean.
- Remove from the water and cool in the refrigerator.

I turn it upside down on a plate to serve it when cooled. You can also fill individual small dishes and cook a little less time. These are nice flipped over on a plate.

Walnut Torte

Preheat Oven to 350°

Line two 8" Cake Pans with Wax Paper. Grease the paper.

3 1/4	Cup Ground Walnuts (Use the Processor)
2	Tablespoons Flour
1	Teaspoon Baking Powder
1/4	Teaspoon Salt
6	Eggs at Room Temperature, separated
1	Cup Sugar
1	Cup Whipping Cream

- Combine the dry ingredients and set aside
- In a small bowl beat the Egg Yolks with the Sugar until lemony.
- Beat the Egg Whites in a large bowl until soft peaks form.
- Gently fold the dry ingredients into the whites. Then fold the Yolk mix gently into the Whites.
- Put into Prepared Pans and Bake for 25 to 30 minutes.
- Cool for 5 minutes and top with Whipped Cream.

You can flavor the Whipped Cream if you want. Serves 8

Chocolate Angel Food Cake

Gretchen Reese – Atlanta

Angel Food Cake (A bought Cake does well here or a mix made up which I prefer).

12	Ounces Chocolate Chips
2	Tablespoons Sugar (Optional)
3	Egg Whites
1/8	Teaspoon Cream of Tartar
1/2	Teaspoon Vanilla
20	Ounces Cool Whip or 2 1/2 Pints Heavy Cream, whipped

- Melt Chips and Cool.

Beat Egg Whites with Cream of Tartar and Vanilla until stiff. Stir in the melted Chocolate.

- Fold in the Cool Whip or Whipped Cream.
- Tear the Angel Food Cake into pieces and fold into Chocolate Cream mixture.
- Put into pretty dish or individual dishes and chill. Top with toasted Almonds.

This will serve 8 or more and is a delicious easy dessert. One time I made this and put in 3/4 Teaspoon of Cream of Tartar. Needless to say we couldn't eat it!

Short Cake Biscuits

Jean Fisher – Atlanta

These are the best I have ever tasted!

Preheat Oven to 450°
Sift Together:

4	Cups Flour
6	Teaspoons Sugar
5	Teaspoons Baking Powder
2	Teaspoons Salt

- Cut 12 Tablespoons Chilled Butter into Pieces.
- Add to Flour Mix and Cut into Flour until it resembles Oatmeal.
- Stir into Flour Butter mix 1 1/2 Cups Heavy Cream until soft balls form.
- Turn out on floured board and knead a bit.
- Roll dough to 1" thick. Cut with biscuit cutter.
- Bake on a cookie sheet for 12 to 15 minutes.

The number of biscuits will vary depending on the size of the cutter.

Slice when cooled. Butter if desired.

Serve with smashed Berries inside and Whipped Cream with sliced Berries over all.

This is a true Strawberry Short Cake. It's great with sliced peaches, too, when they are in season.

Apple Raspberry Crumble

Martha Stewart Quick Cook

Heat oven to 375°

3	Granny Smith Apples
	Juice of 1 Lemon
1	10 ounce Container Frozen Berries or 1 Pint Fresh Berries
1	Cup Flour
1/2	Cup Sugar
1/2	Cup (1 stick) Unsalted Butter
1/4	Teaspoon Nutmeg
	Heavy Cream

- Peel and Core Apples. Cut into 8 or 10 slices.
- Arrange in a buttered baking dish and sprinkle with Lemon Juice.
- Drain Raspberries and sprinkle over apples. (Martha says to save juice for another use).
- Mix Flour and Sugar in a bowl. Cut in Butter with your fingers until mixture is crumbly.
- Add Nutmeg and Cover Fruit with crumble.
- Bake for 25 minutes until the top is golden brown. Serve with Whipped Cream.

This is an easy great dessert and I usually serve it with Ice Cream. Serves 8.

Lemon Sponge Cups

From the Barranquilla Days

Heat Oven to 350°

You need 6 greased custard cups and a pan of boiling water to set them in.

2	Tablespoons Butter
1	Cup Sugar
4	Tablespoons Flour
1-1/2	Cups Milk
1/4	Teaspoons Lemon Juice
	Grated Rind of 1 Lemon
3	Eggs, separated

- Cream Butter. Add Sugar, Flour, Salt, Lemon Juice, and Lemon Rind.
- Beat Egg Yolks well and mix with Milk. Add to creamed mixture.
- Pour into prepared custard cups and set in a pan of boiling water.
- Bake for 45 minutes.
- When done each cup will have lemon custard on the bottom and sponge cake on the top.
- Cool and unmold. It will make it's own sauce.

Miscellaneous

Chili Sauce

Guatemala Cookbook

- Chop together:

24	Large tomatoes Peeled
8	Onions
10	Green Peppers

- Put in Large Pot.
- Add:

4	Tablespoons Salt
6	Cups Sugar
6	Cups Cider Vinegar
1 1/2	Teaspoons Ground Cloves
1 1/2	Teaspoons Alspice
2	Teaspoons Cinnamon

- Cook together several hours until thick. Stir gently occasionally.
- Makes 9 pints.

This is great on everything including eggs. It makes a nice Christmas gift with a pretty top.

Hot Curried Fruit

Heat oven to 325°

1	29 Ounce Can Peach Halves, Drained
1	29 Ounce Can Pear Halves, Drained
1	29 Ounce Can Pineapple Chunks, Drained
2	17 Ounce Cans Apricot Halves, Drained

- Place the Fruits in a 13" x 9" x 2" baking dish.
- Combine:

1/2	Cup Butter, Softened
1	Cup Brown Sugar, Packed
1	Tablespoon Corn Starch
1	Teaspoon Curry Powder

- Spoon over the Fruit.
- Bake for 1 hour basting occasionally with liquid.
- Serve with slotted spoon.

It is great with Poultry and Pork. It can be used as a dessert, too. Serve it over Ice Cream or Pound Cake or both.

Christmas Salad Dressing

Makes about 3 Cups

1	10 Ounce Can Tomato soup, Undiluted
1/3	Cup Honey
	Pinch of Salt
1	Tablespoon Paprika
2	Teaspoons Prepared Mustard
2	Tablespoons Chopped Onion
1/4	Cup Lemon Juice
2	Tablespoons White Vinegar
1	Tablespoon Worcestershire
3/4	Cup Vegetable Oil or Olive Oil
1	Garlic Clove, Cut in Half

- Place all ingredients, except for Oil and Garlic in a blender container and blend at high speed.
- With blender still running gradually add the oil. Continue to blend until well combined.
- Pour the Dressing into a container with a tight fitting lid and add Garlic.
- Cover and refrigerate. Use as needed.

It's called Christmas because of the color, but it's good all year round.

Chinese Mustard

Betty Bono – Guatemala

1	Tablespoon Dry Mustard
1	Tablespoon Vinegar
1/2	Cup Ketchup
1/4	Teaspoon Curry
1/2	Teaspoon Horse Radish
1	Tablespoon Sugar
1	Clove Minced Garlic
1	Cup Whiskey
1	Tablespoon Ginger

- Mix together well. This keeps in the refrigerator for at least 2 weeks.

This is great for dipping won tons. That is what I served it with at parties. It's also good on Roast Beef and Pork and as a dip for Shrimp.

Barbecue Sauce

2	Tablespoons Olive Oil
1	Medium Onion, Finely Chopped
2	Tablespoons Vinegar
2	Tablespoons Brown Sugar
1/4	Cup Lemon Juice
1	Cup Ketchup
3	Tablespoons Worcestershire
1/2	Tablespoon Prepared Mustard
1	Cup Water
1/2	Cup Celery, Finely Chopped

- Brown the Onion in the Oil.
- Add the remaining ingredients.
- Simmer for 30 minutes.

This is good on the Ribs, Meat, or Chicken. It keeps well in the refrigerator.

Hush Puppies

Henry Williams – Hilton Head, SC

2	Cups corn Meal Mix
1	Tablespoon flour
1	Egg Beaten
3	Tablespoons Chopped Onions (More may be added if you want)
1	Cup Buttermilk

- Drop by spoonful (size depends on you) into hot Oil. Fry until golden brown.
- Drain on Paper towel.

These are usually fried in the Oil that the Fish was Fried in for the best taste. They are delicious and very southern. They are a great addition to a Fish Fry or Fried Chicken meal.

Henry said that the Hush Puppy name came at hunting trips and were used to quiet the Hound "Dawgs." They would throw them one and say "Hush Puppy"! I really liked the story.

www.ingramcontent.com/pod-product-compliance
Lightning Source LLC
Chambersburg PA
CBHW060803150426
42813CB00059B/2870

* 9 7 8 0 9 7 8 9 2 7 1 7 2 *